COUNTRYSID

GW01312350

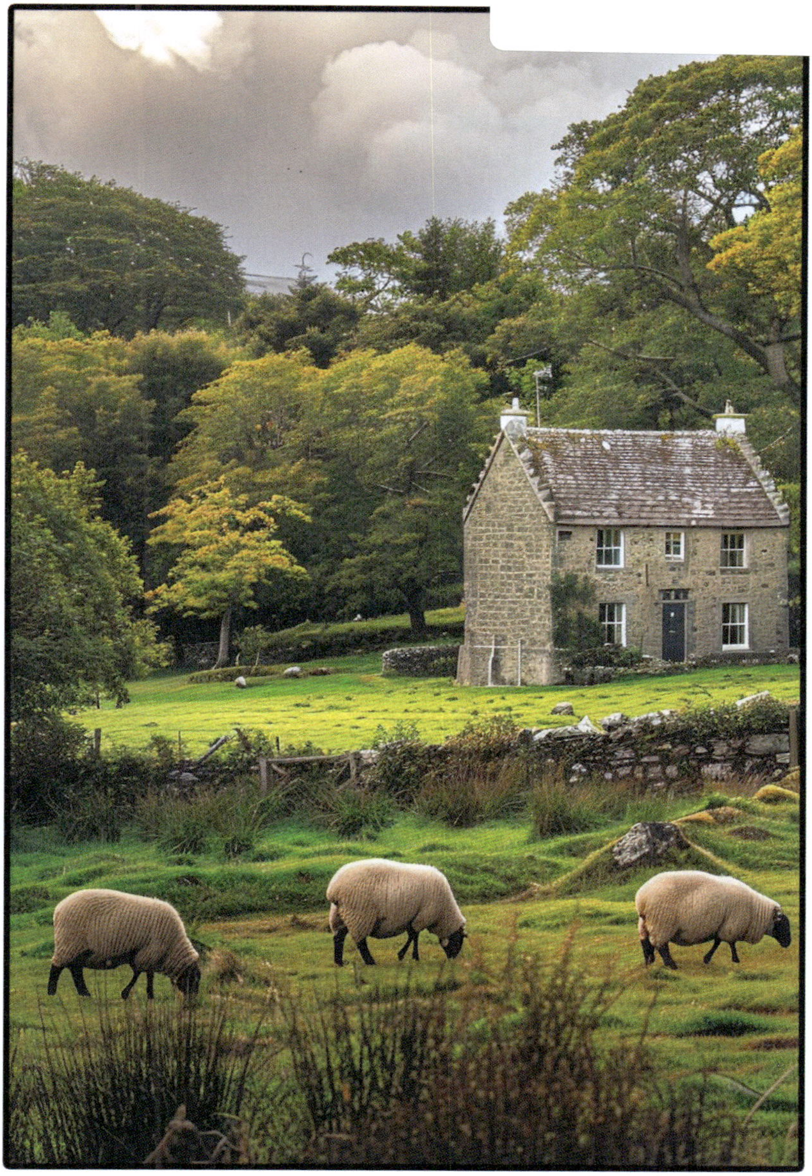

Monica Austin

Copyright 2024 Monica Austin. All rights reserved.

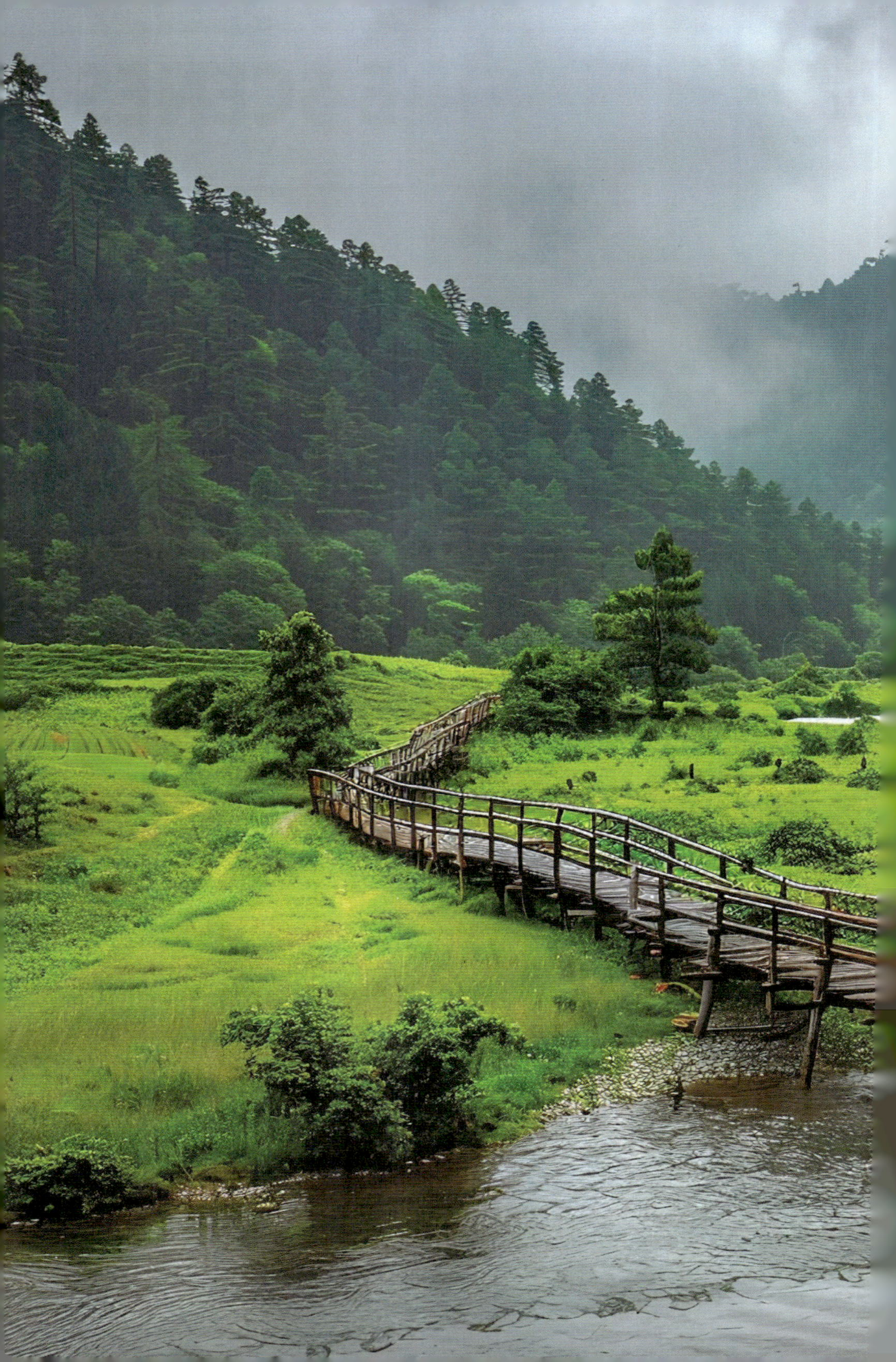

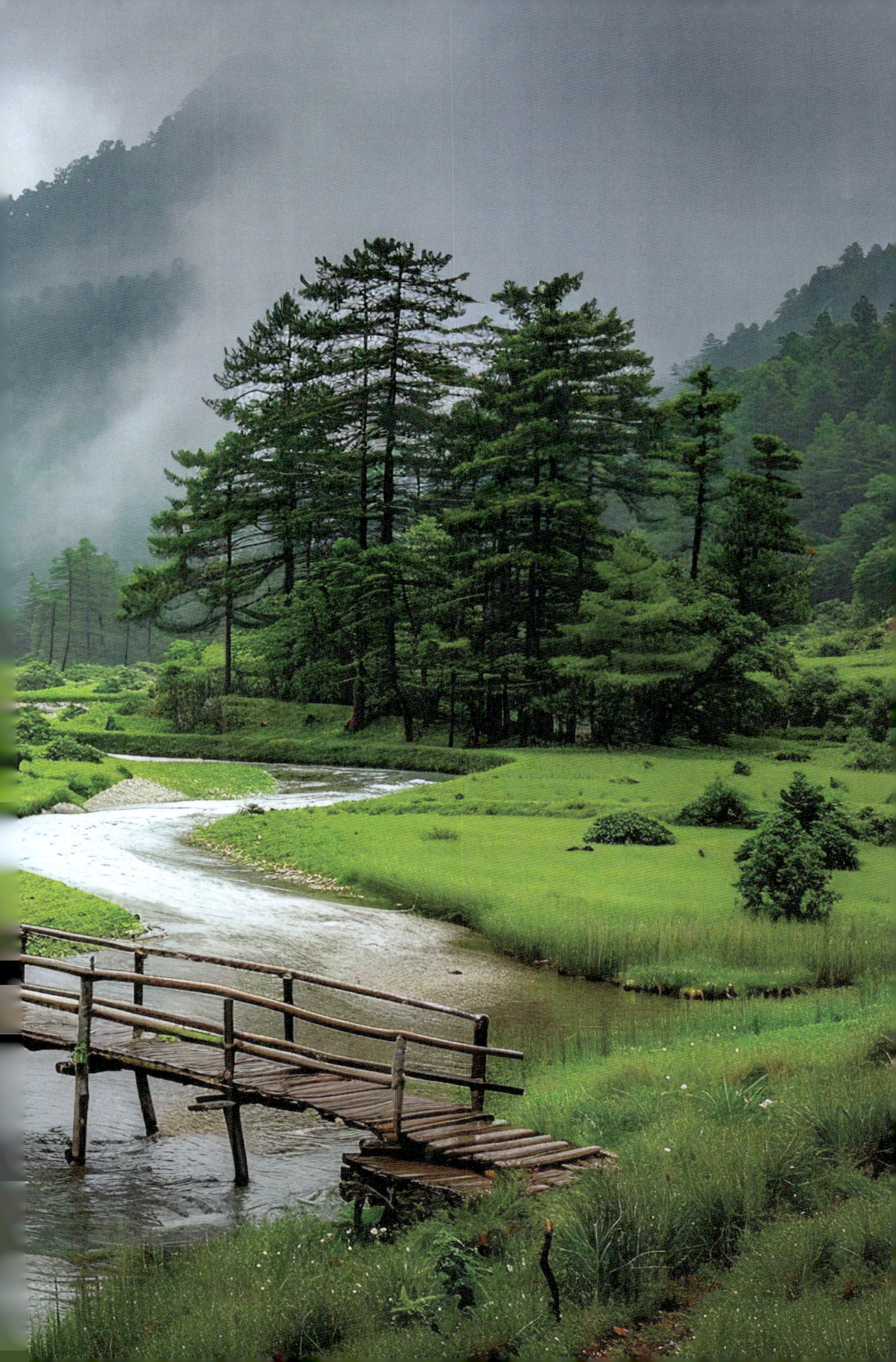

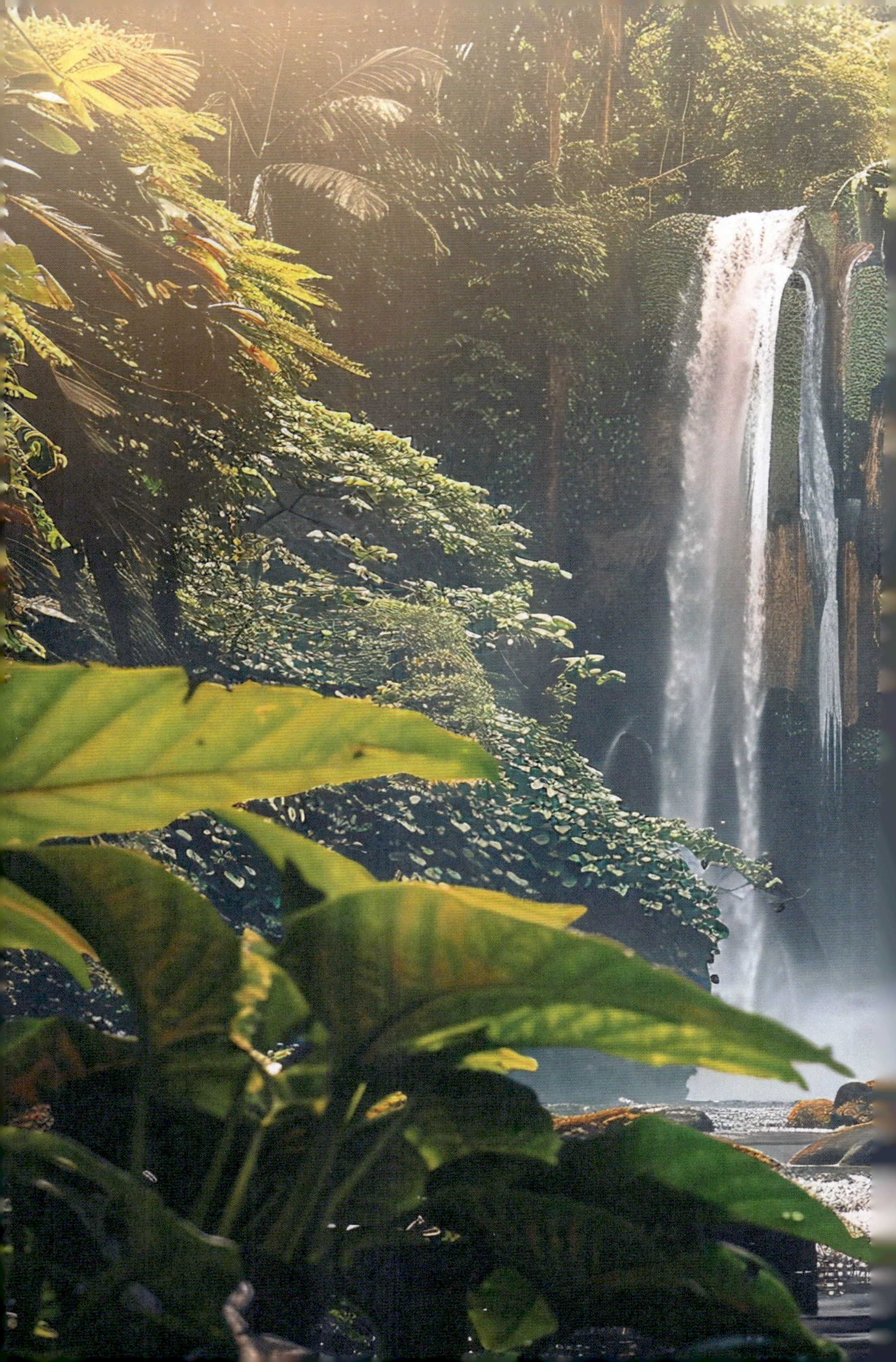

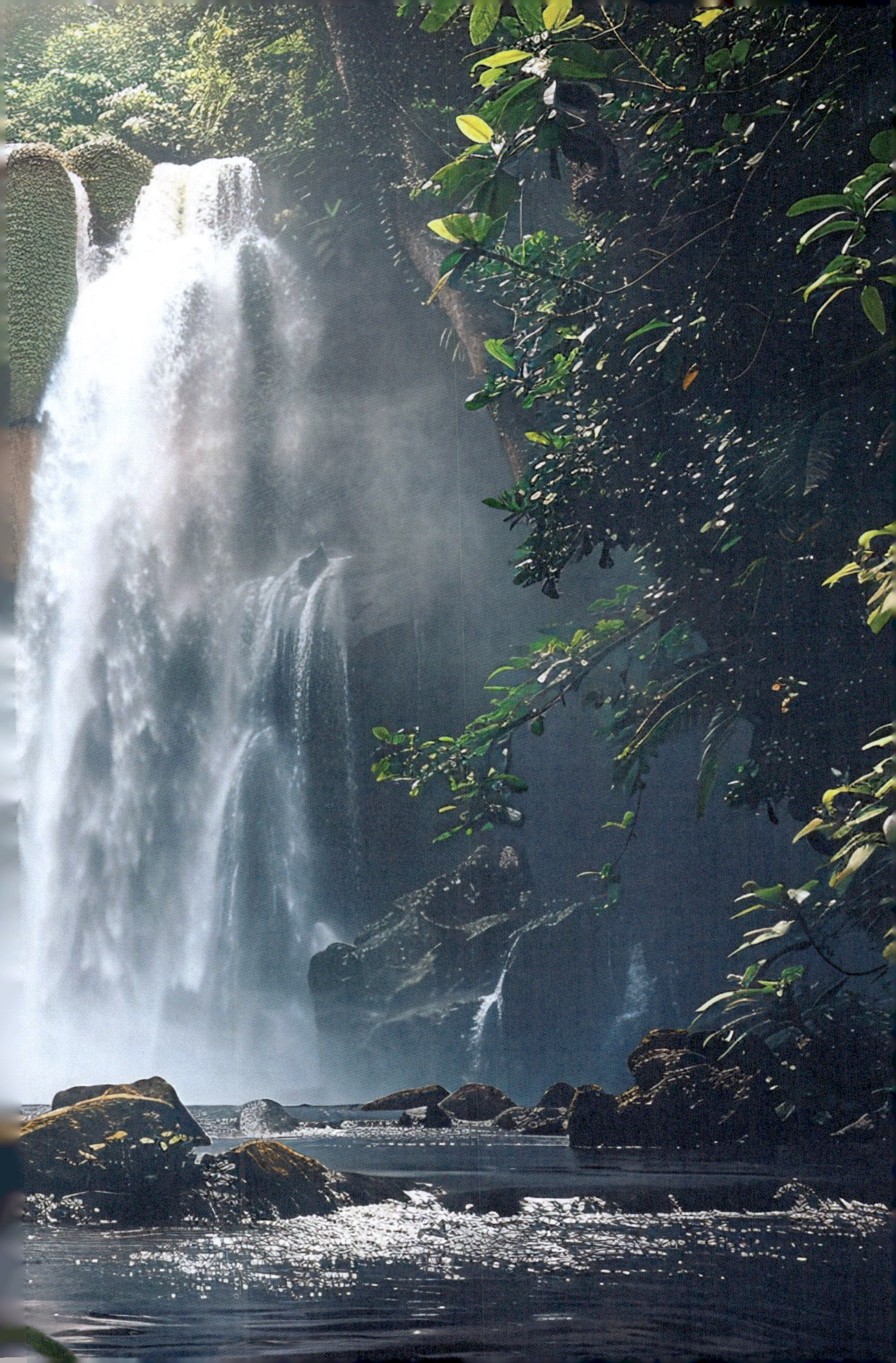

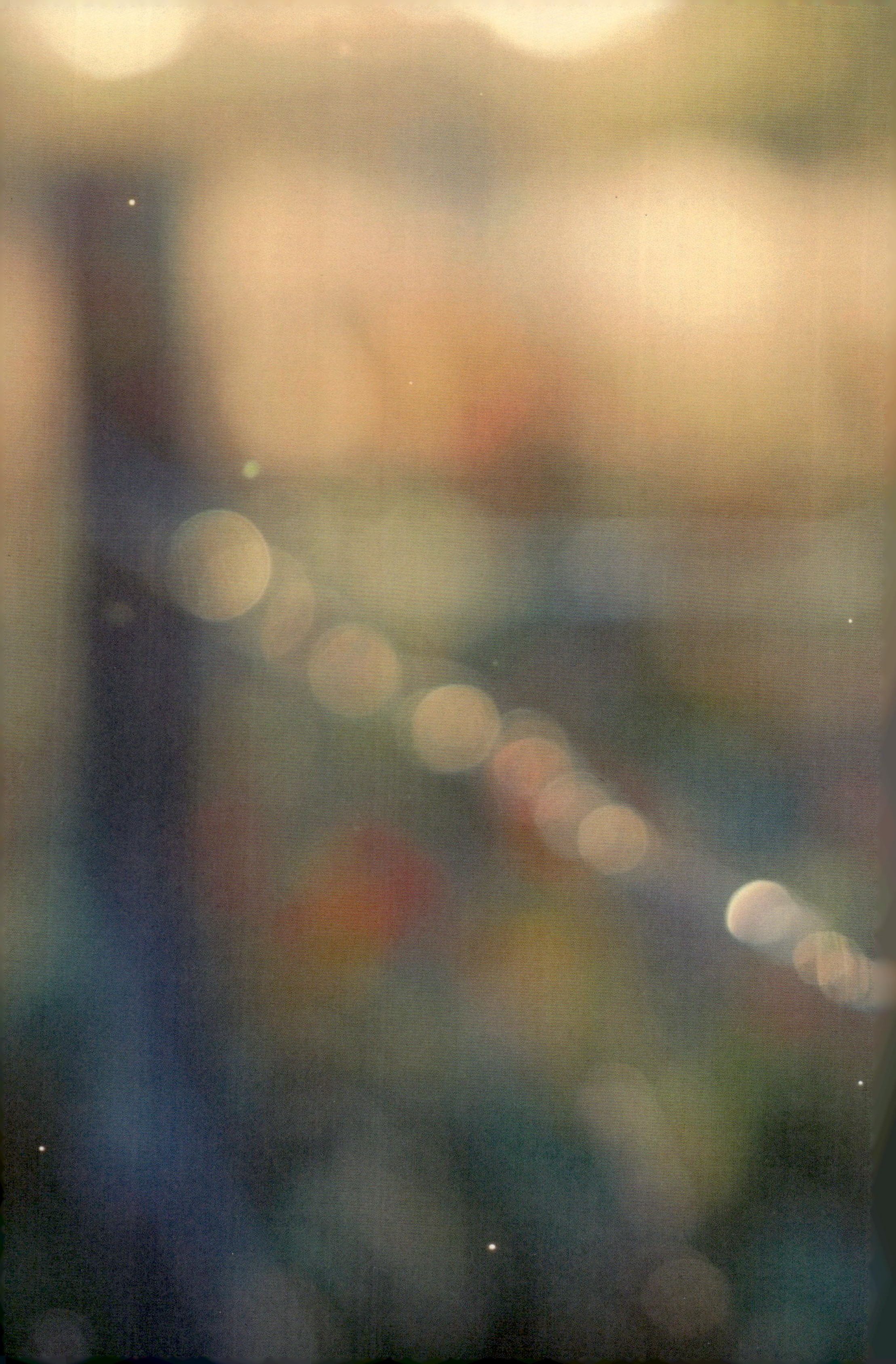

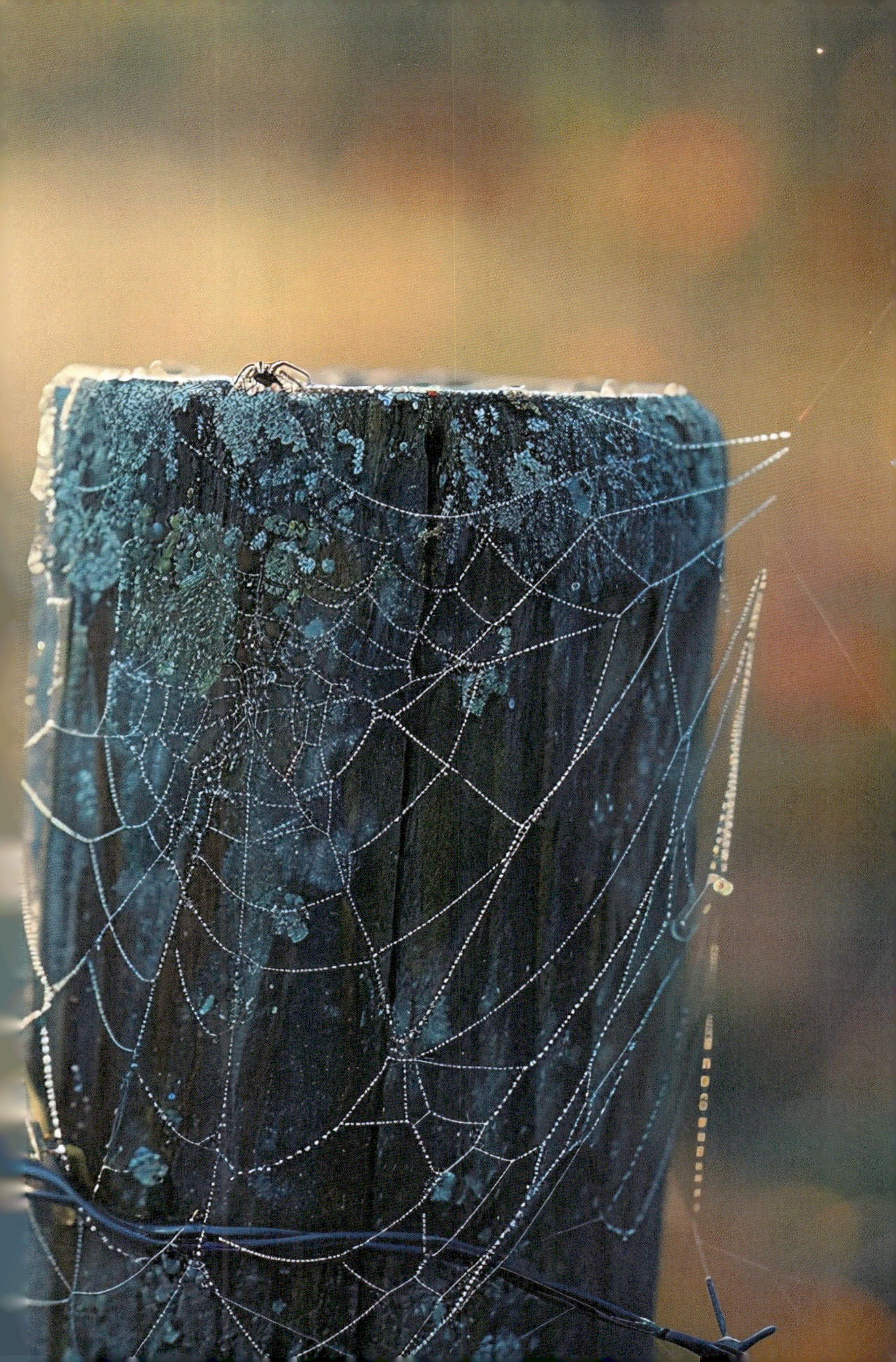

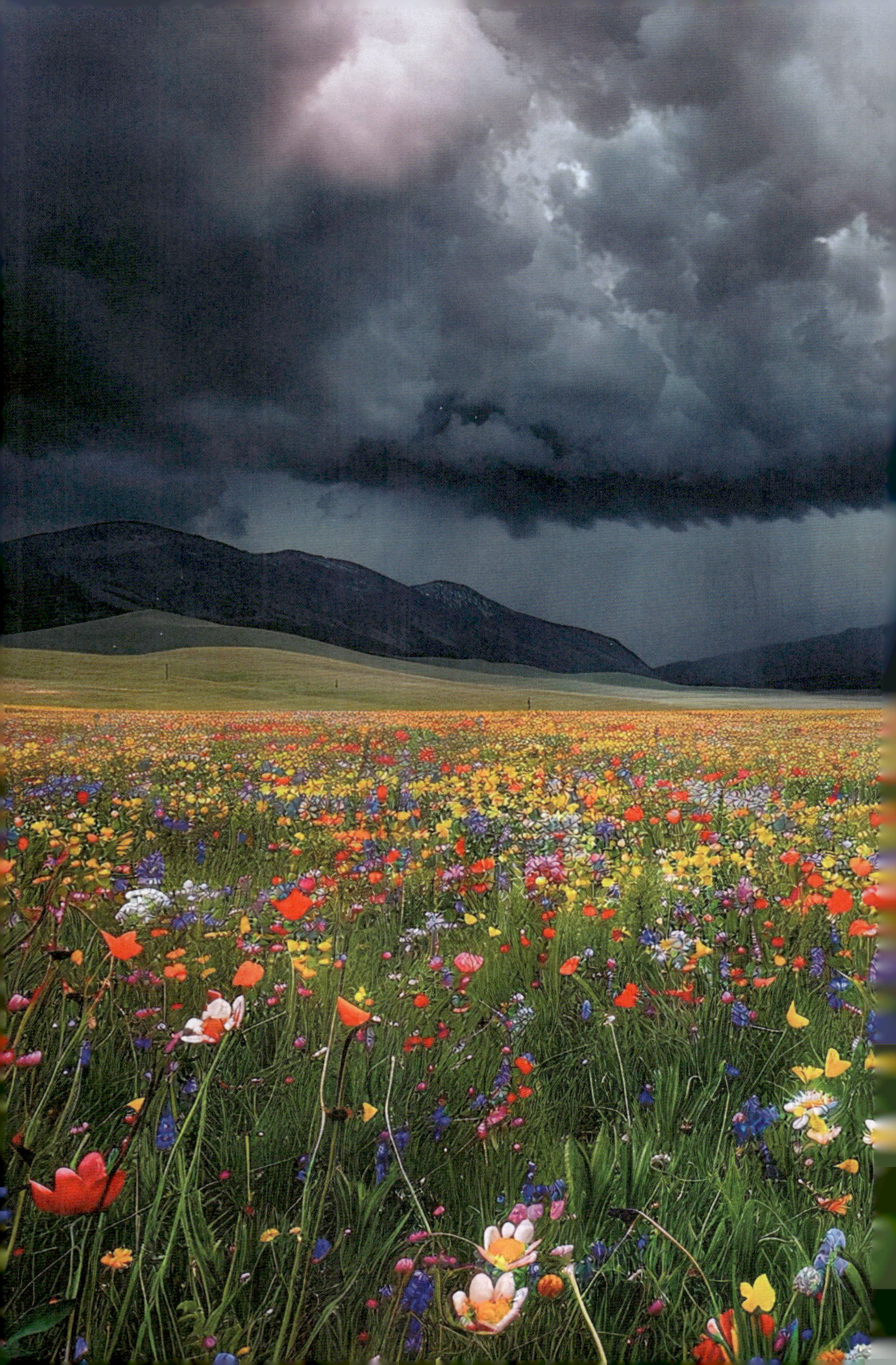

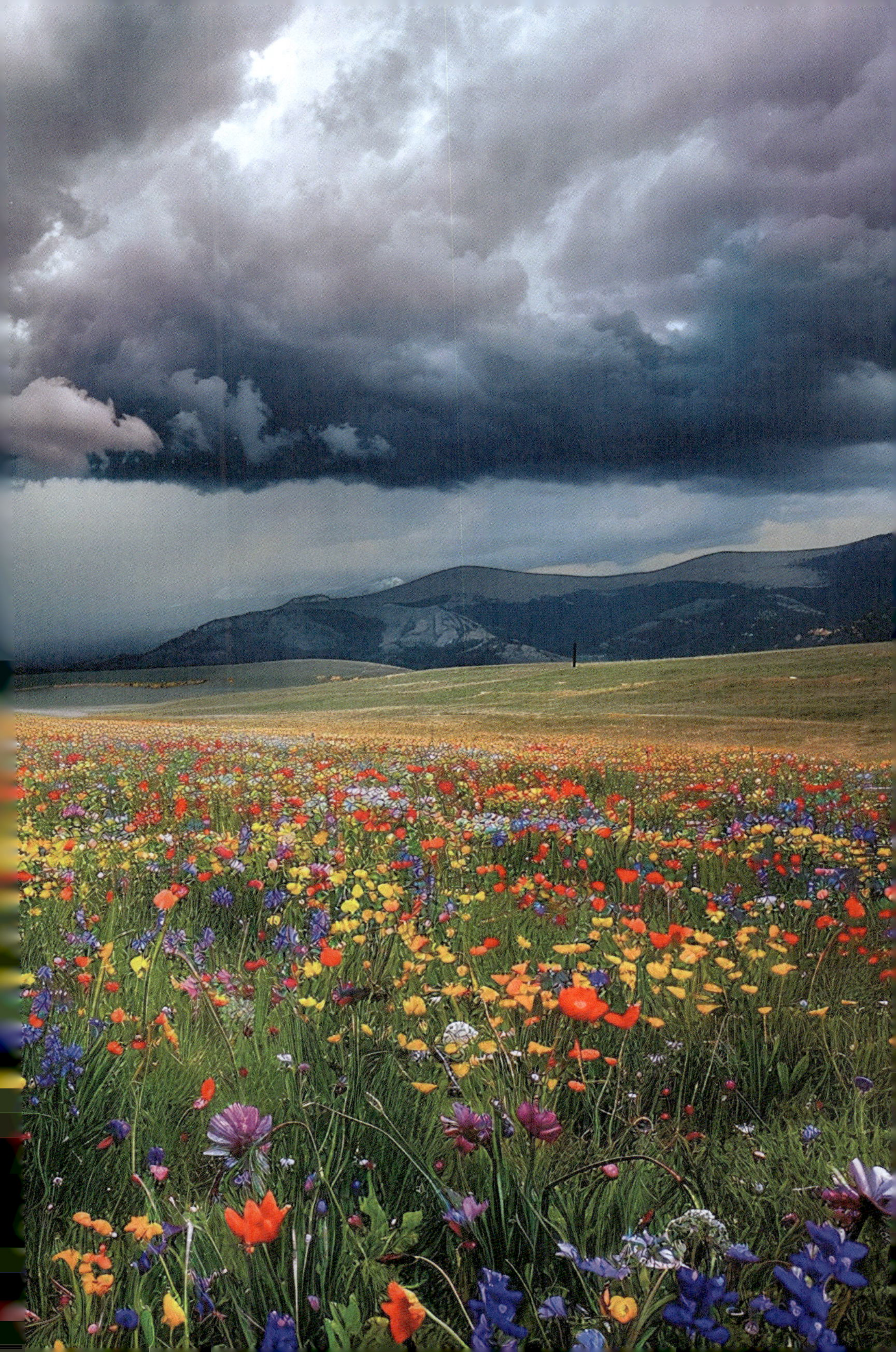

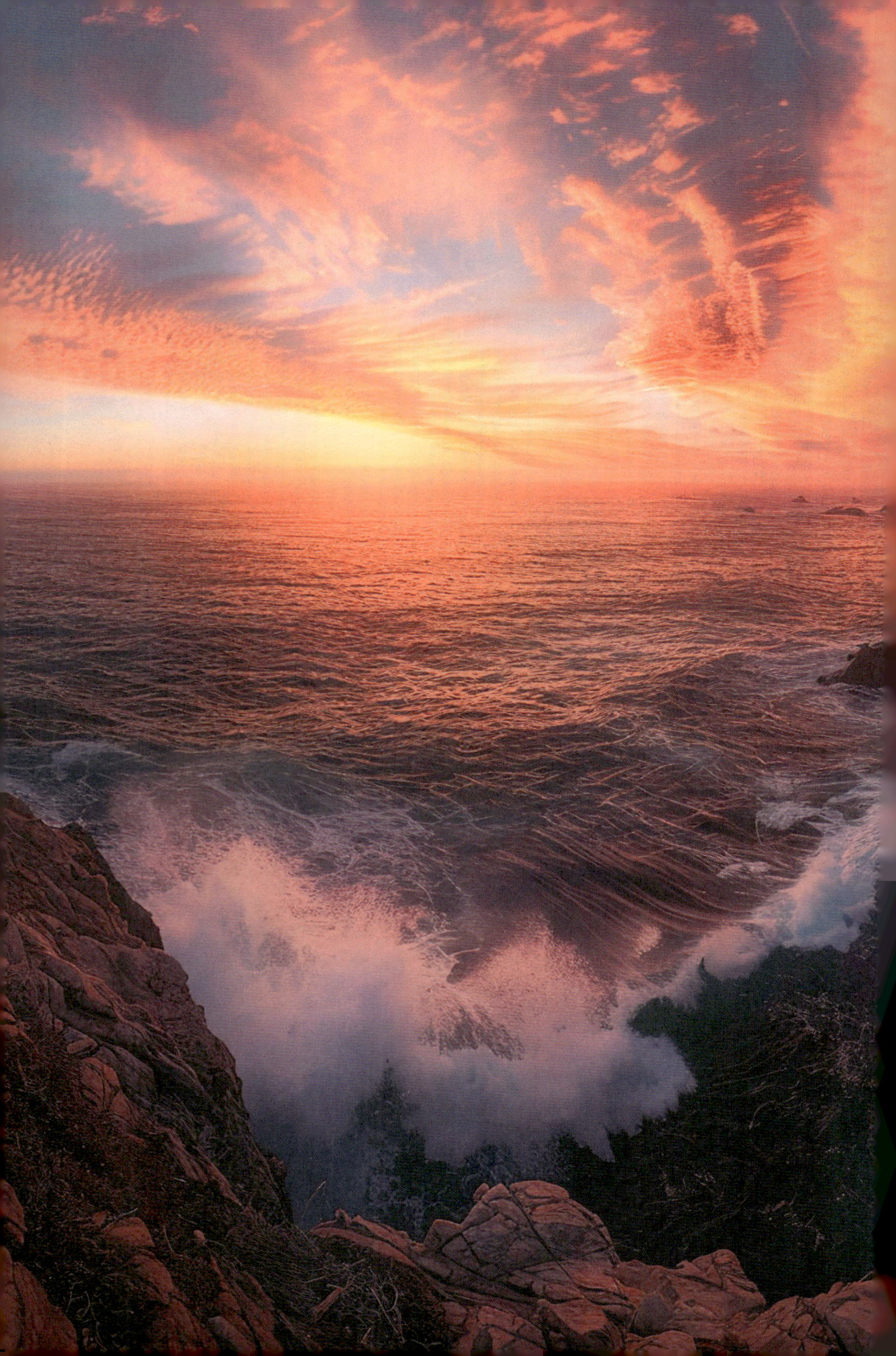

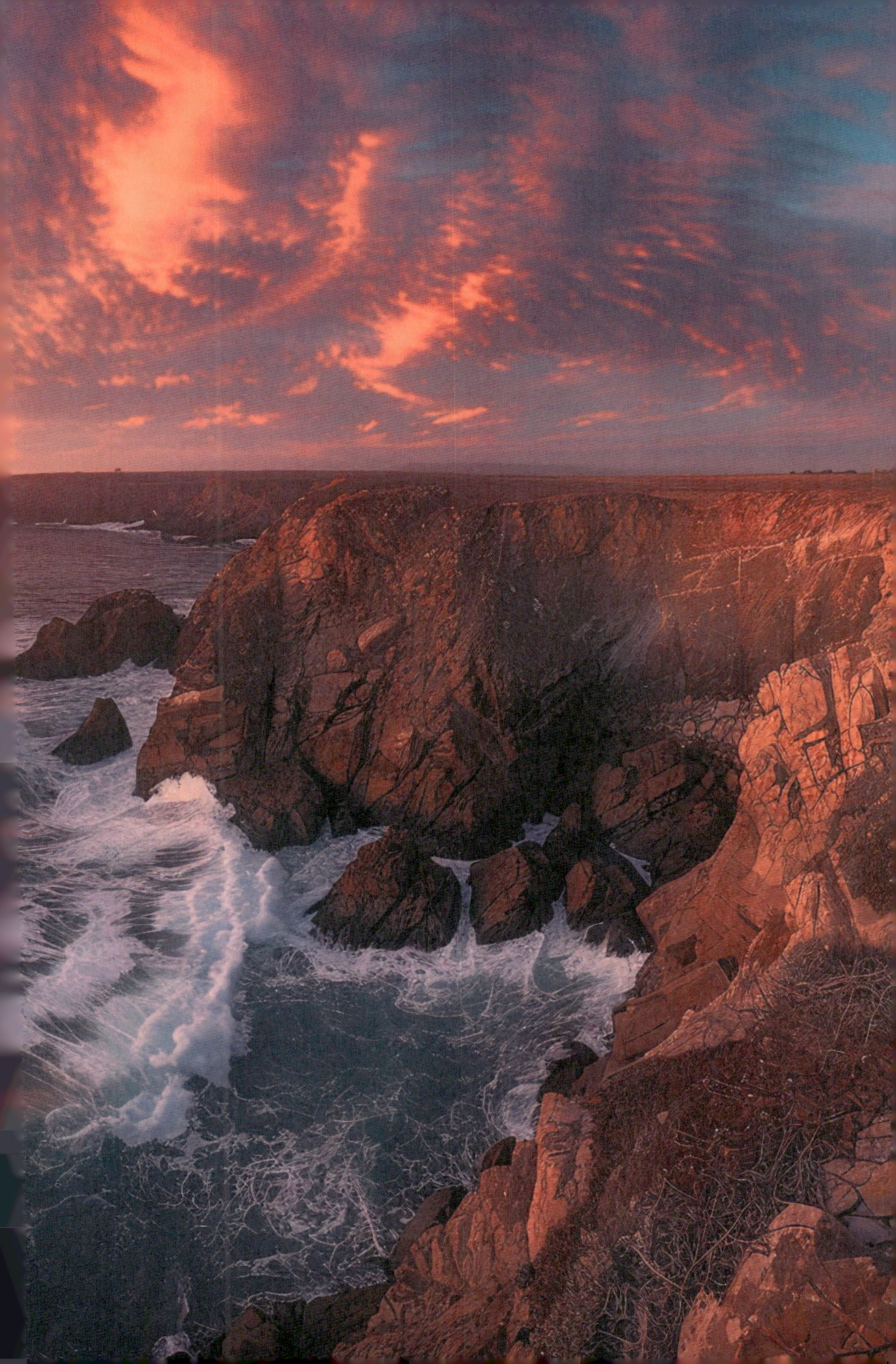

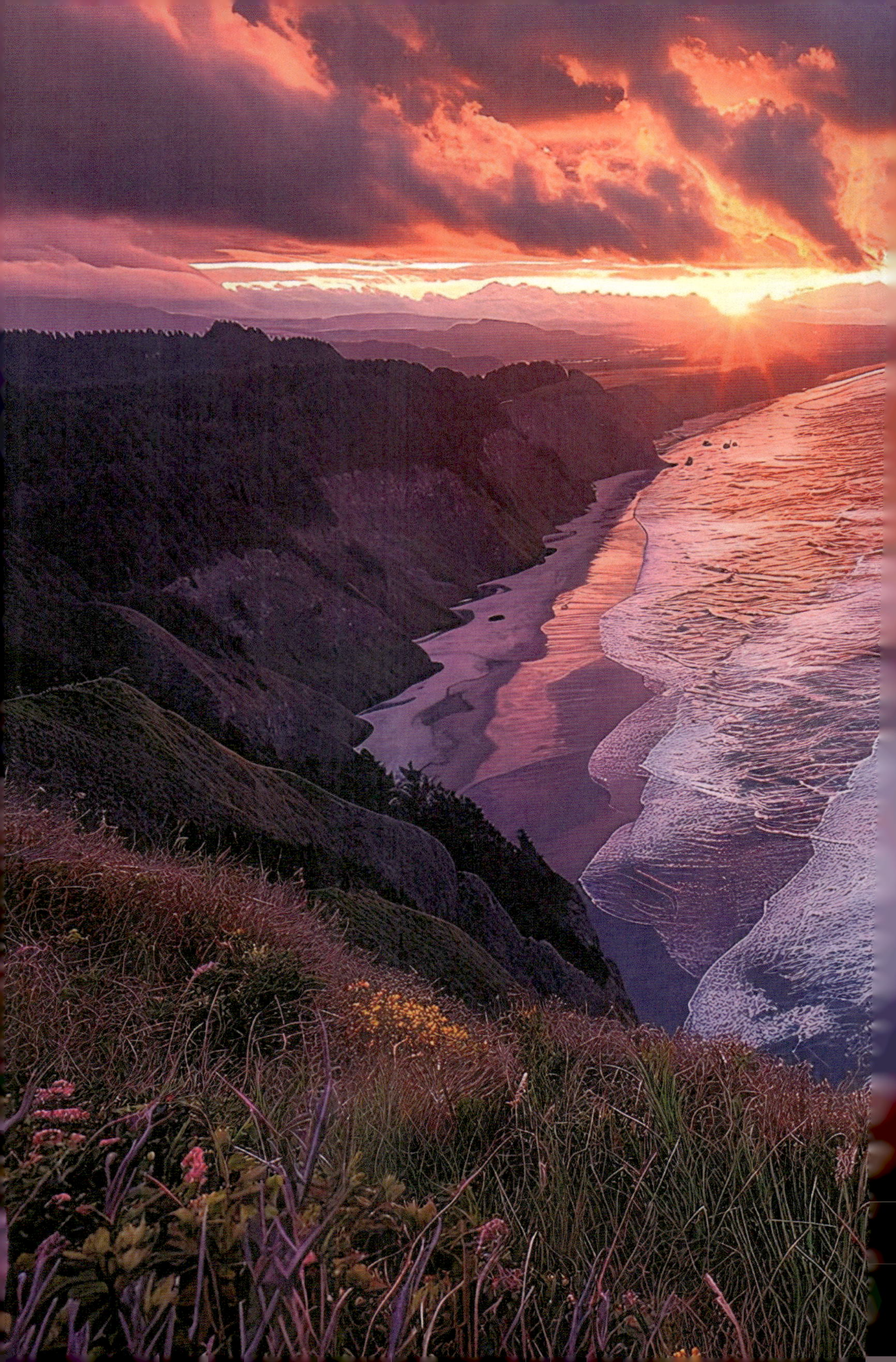

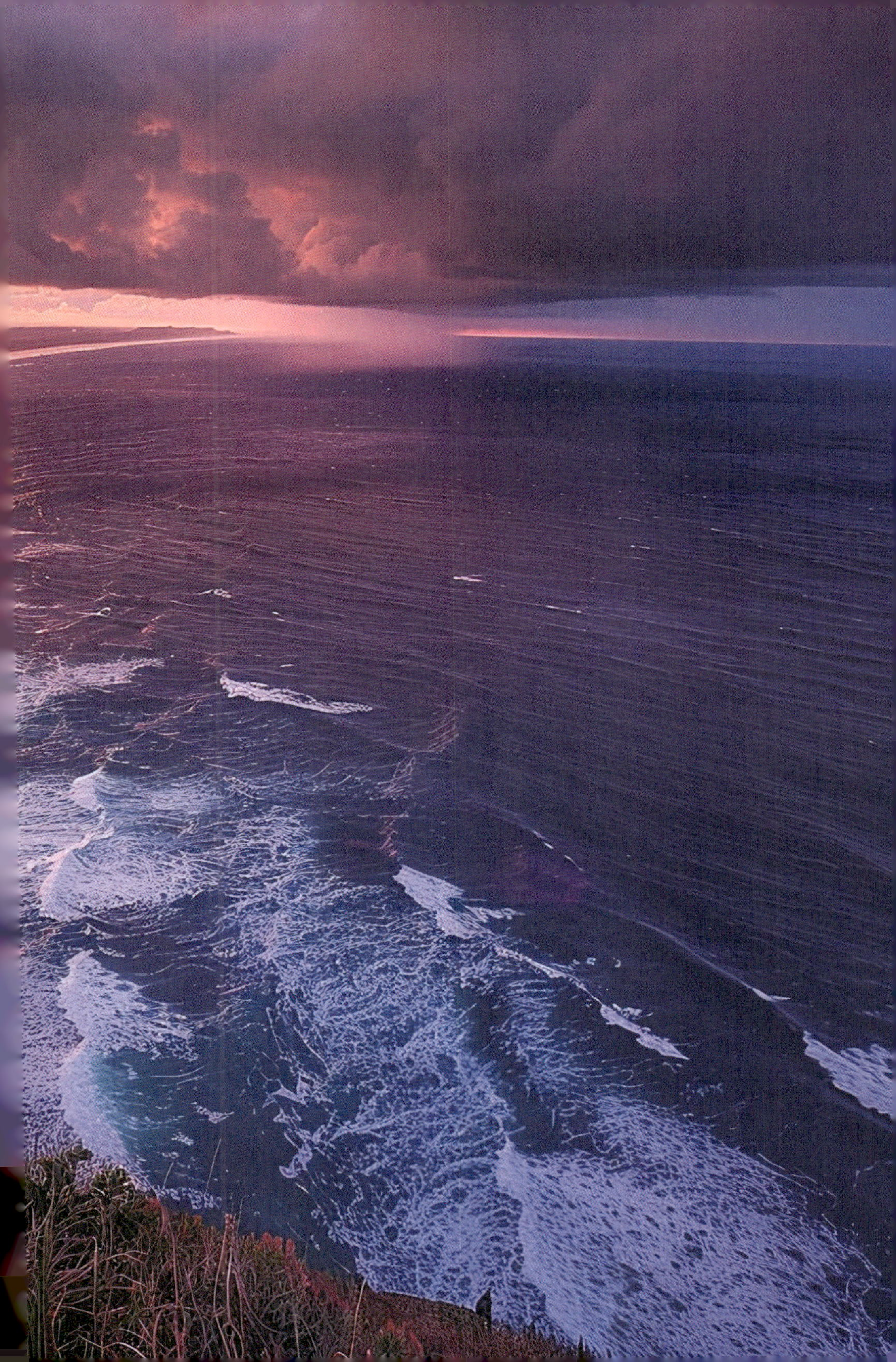

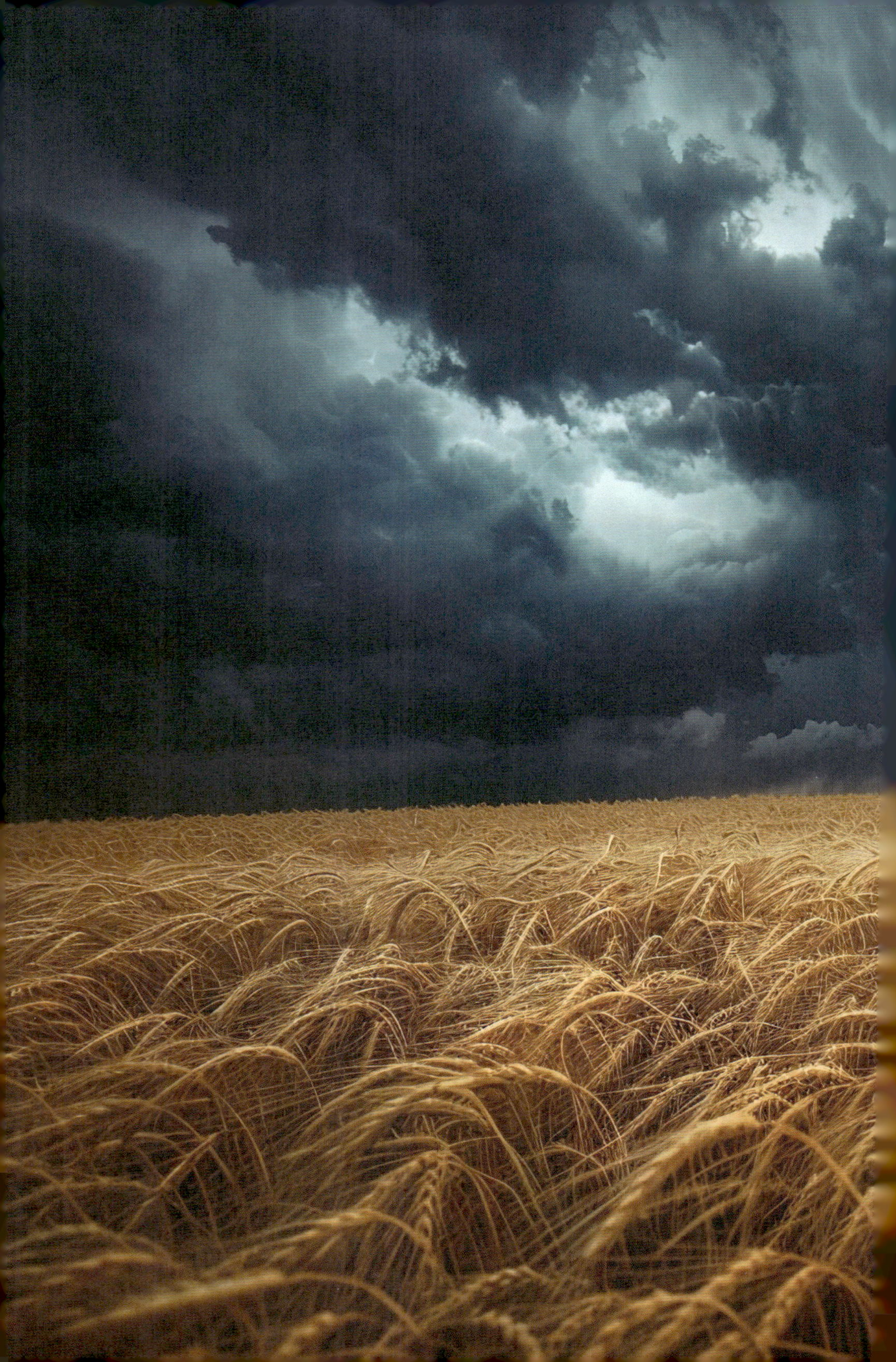

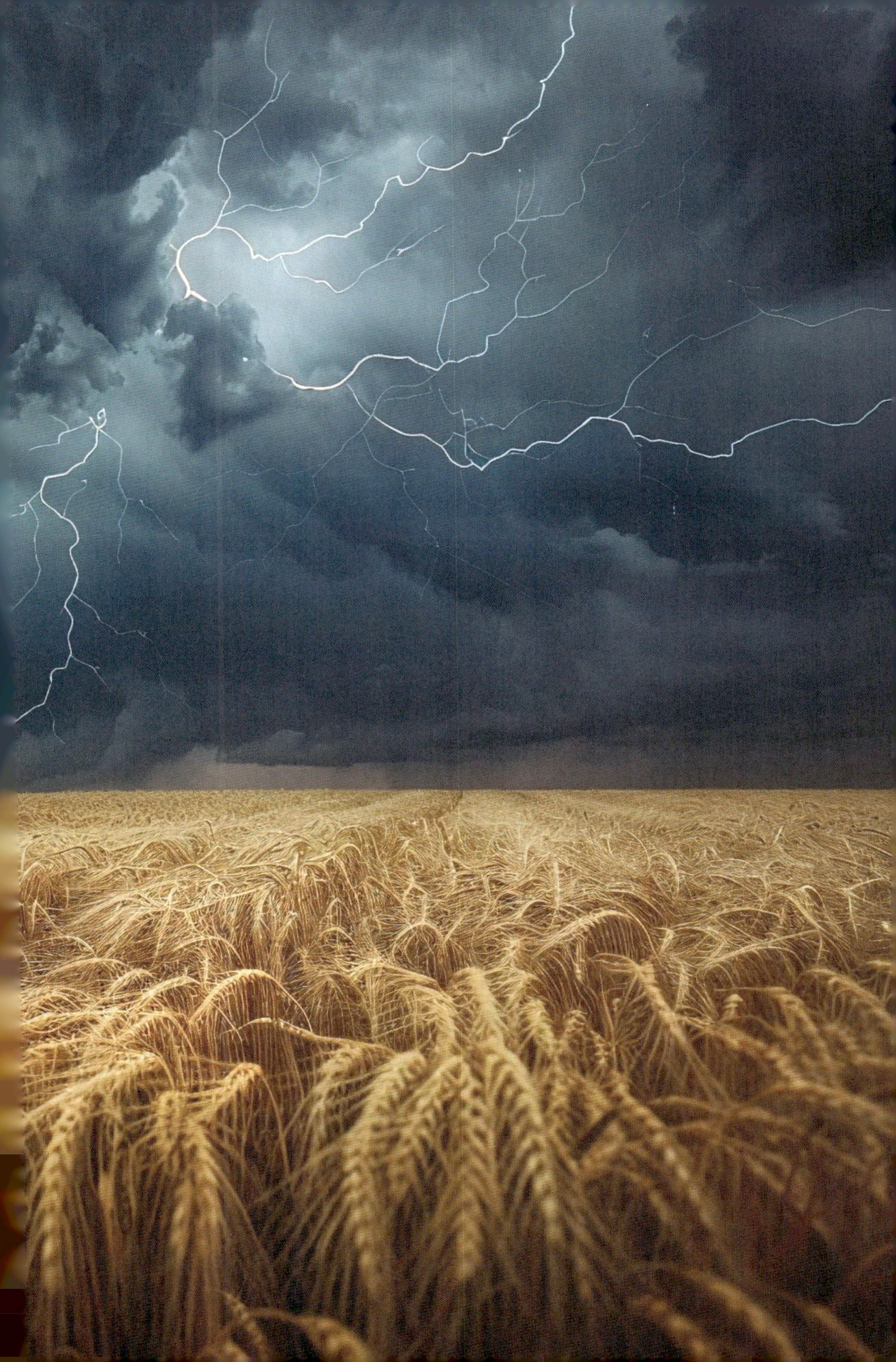

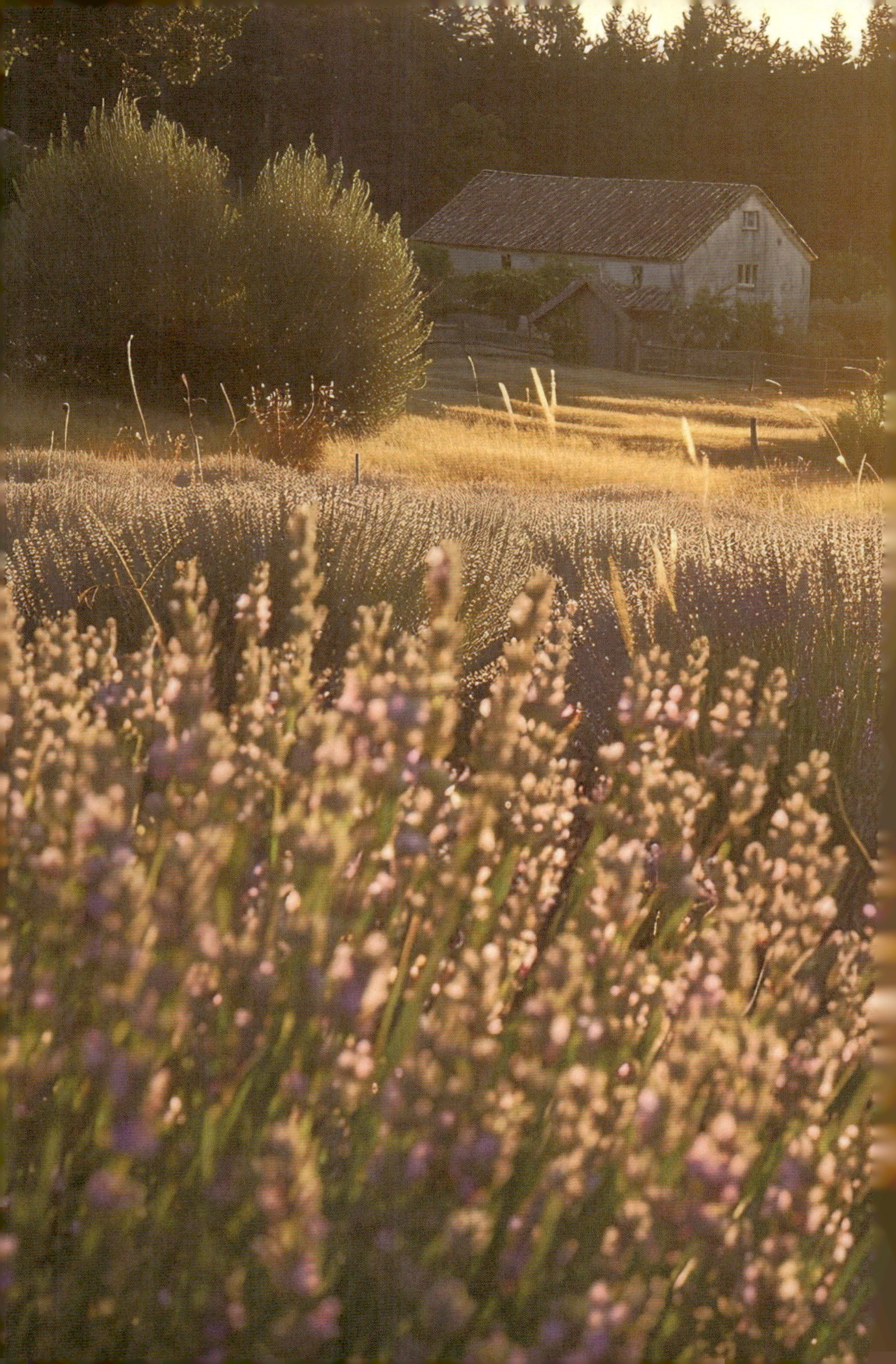

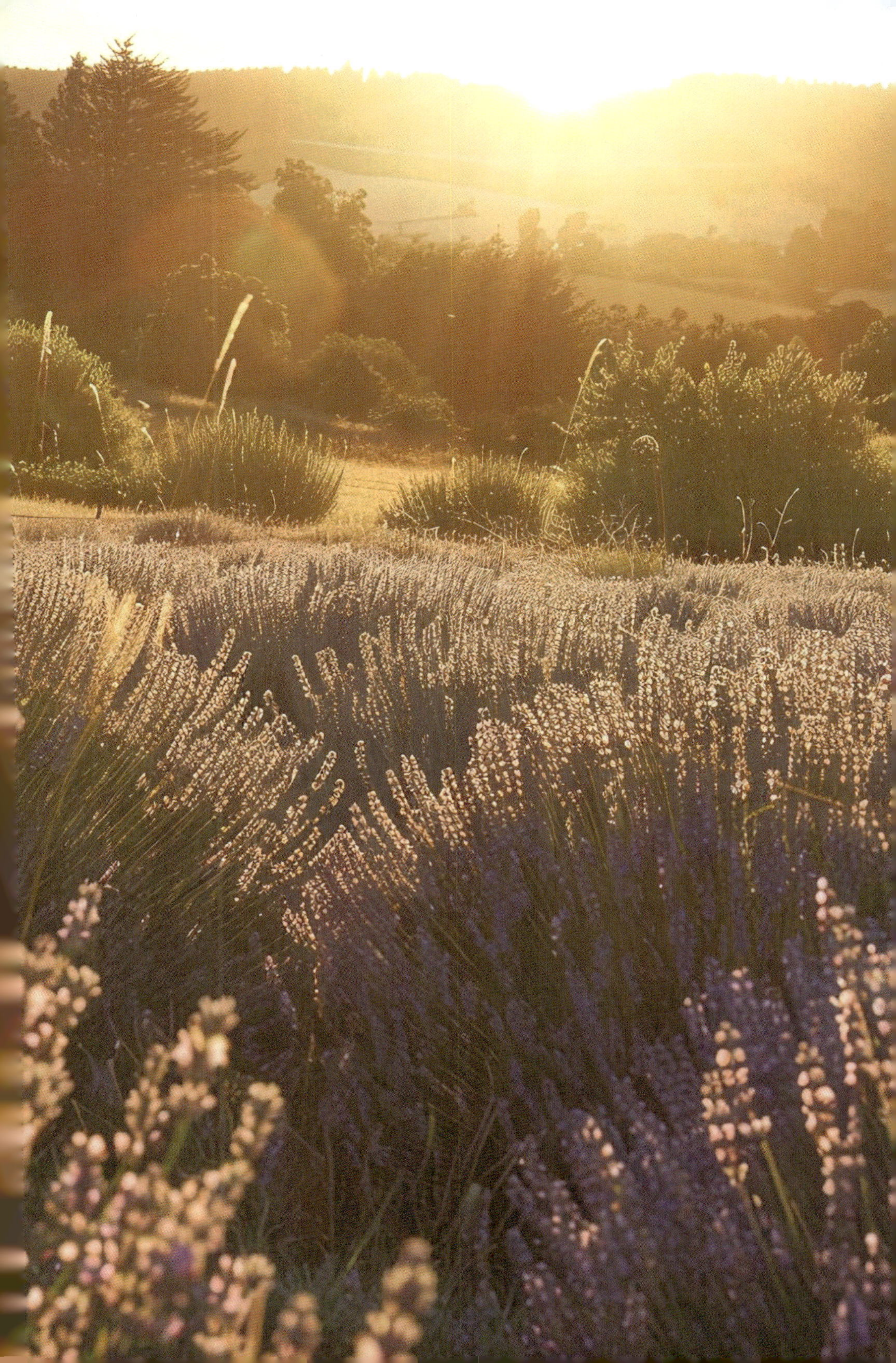

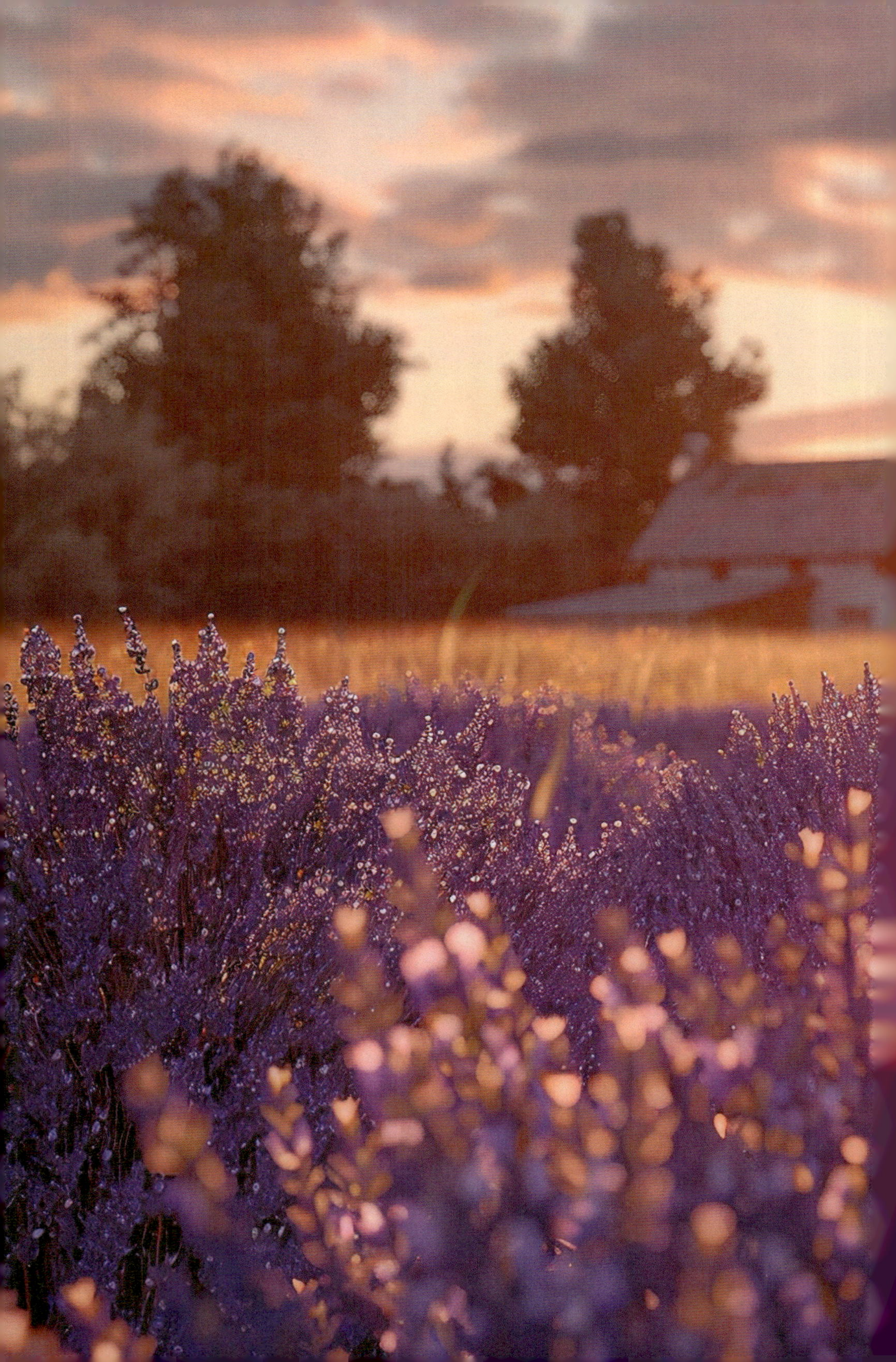

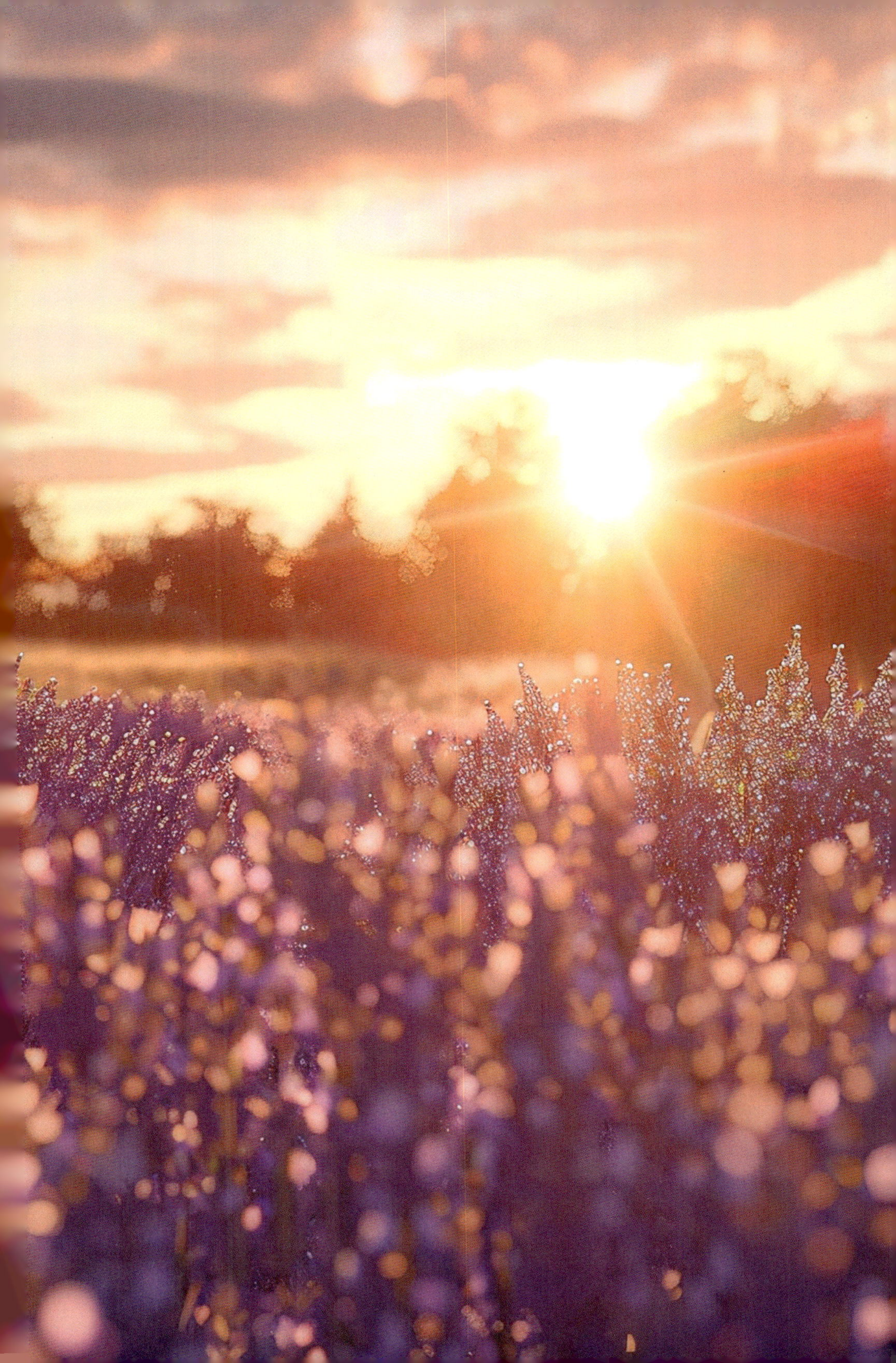

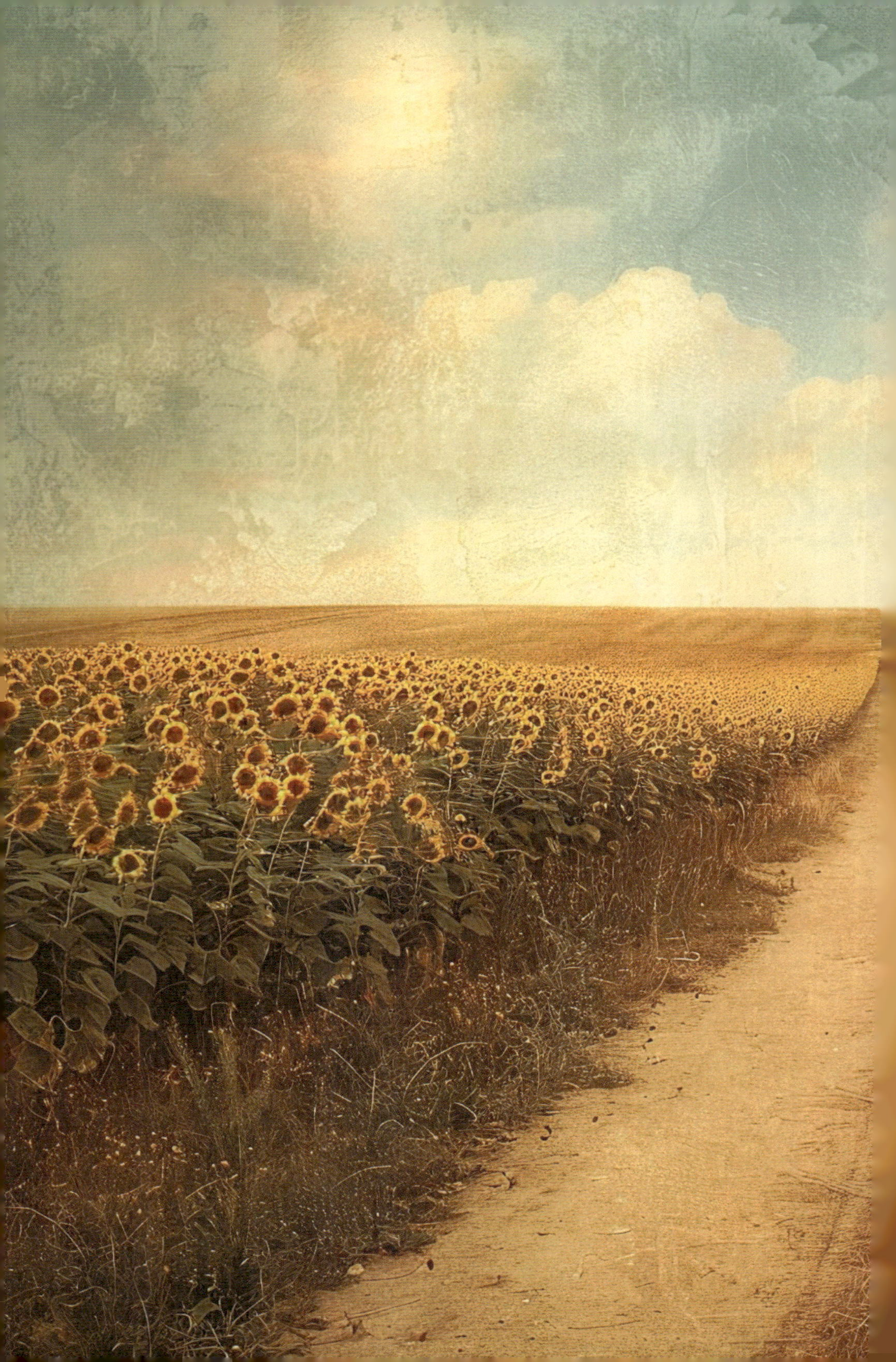

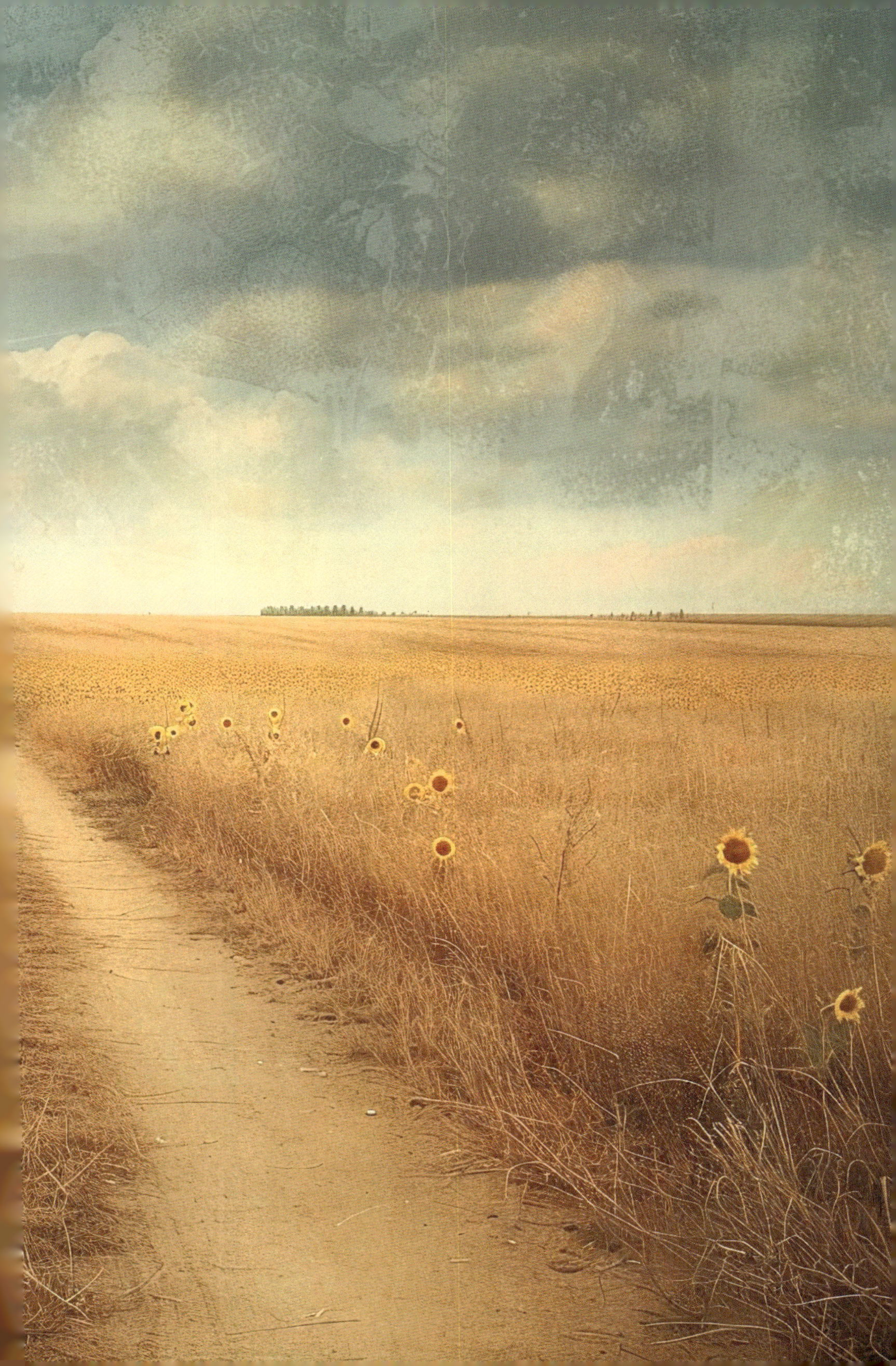

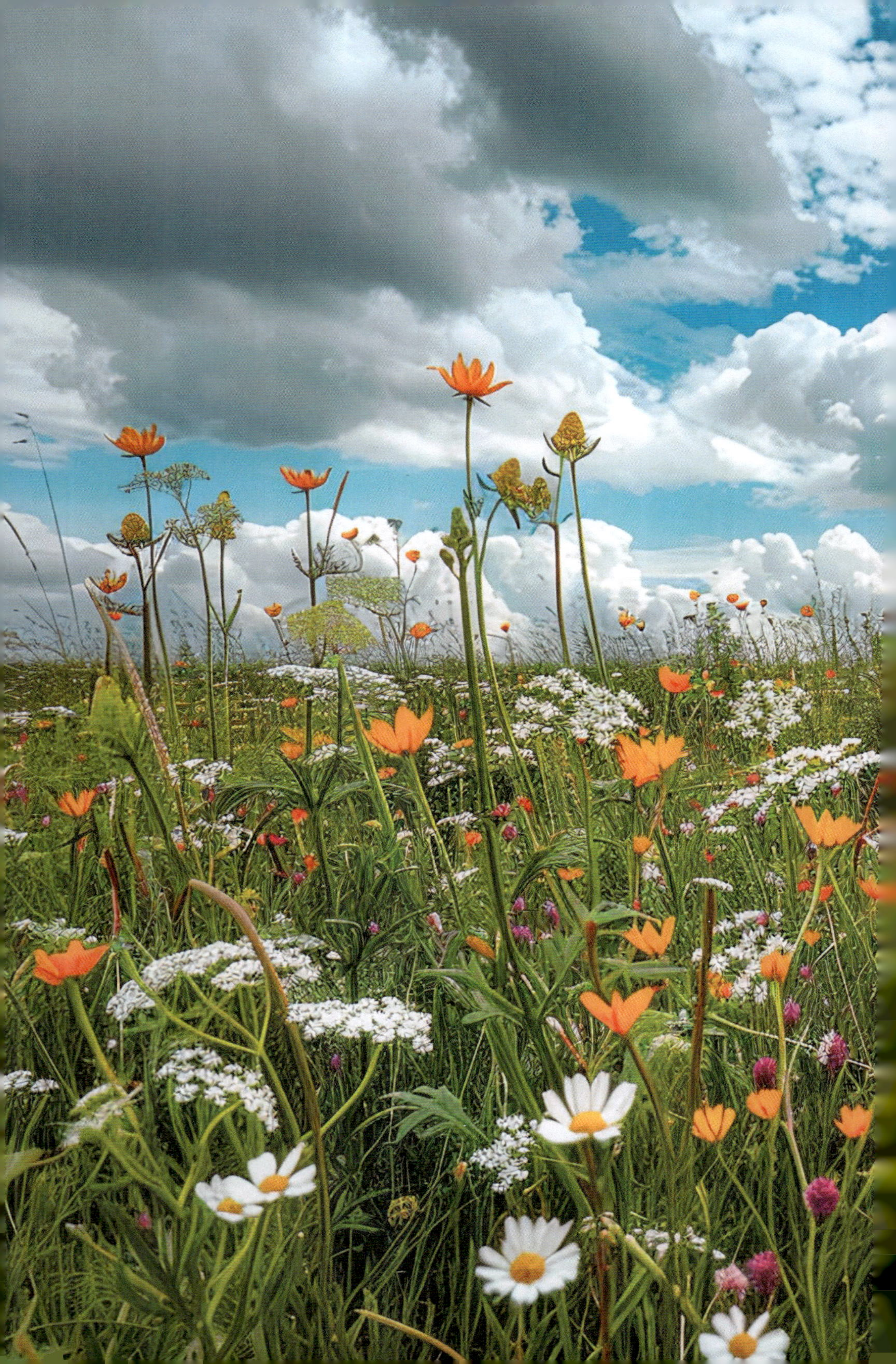

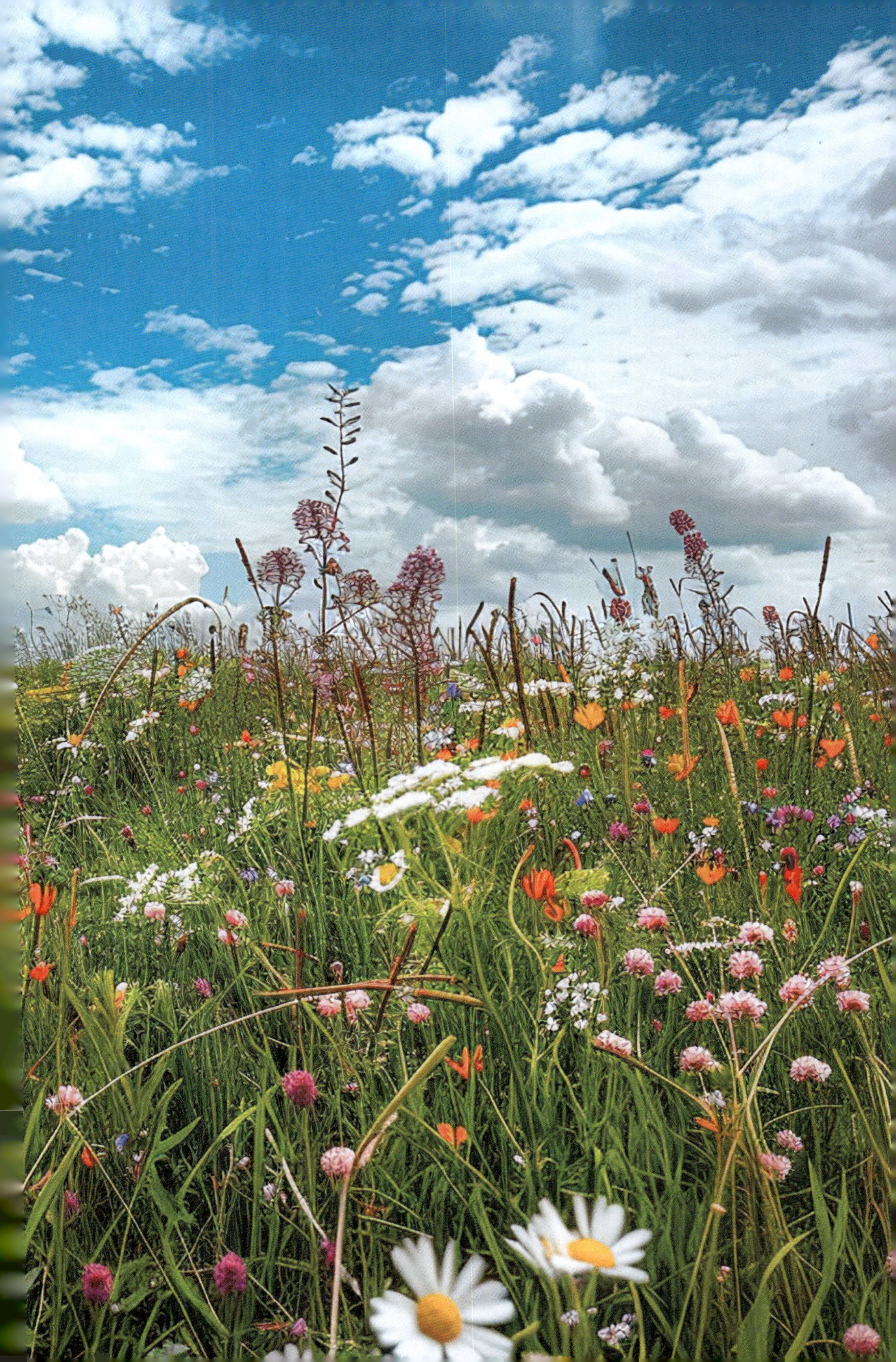

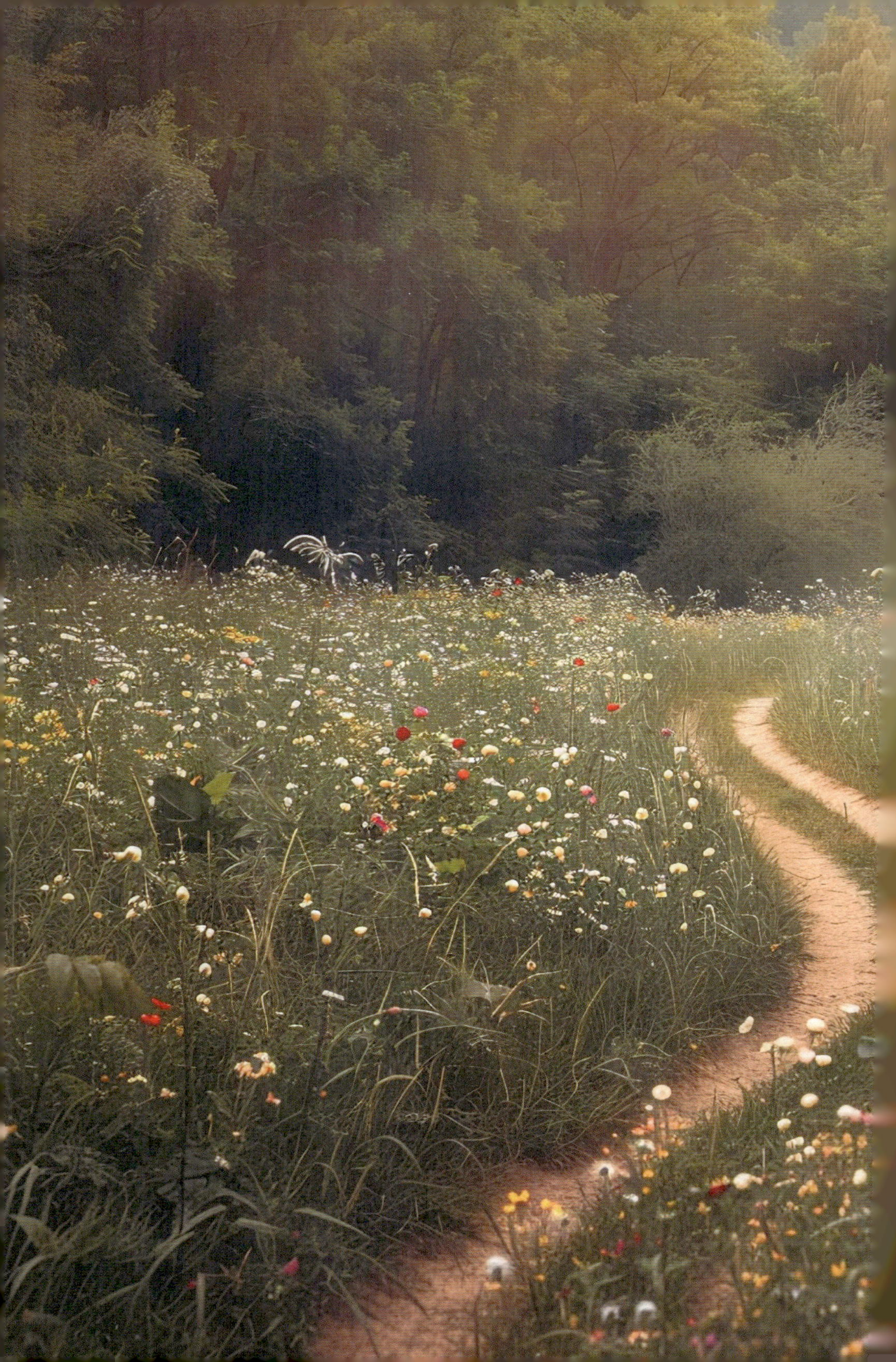

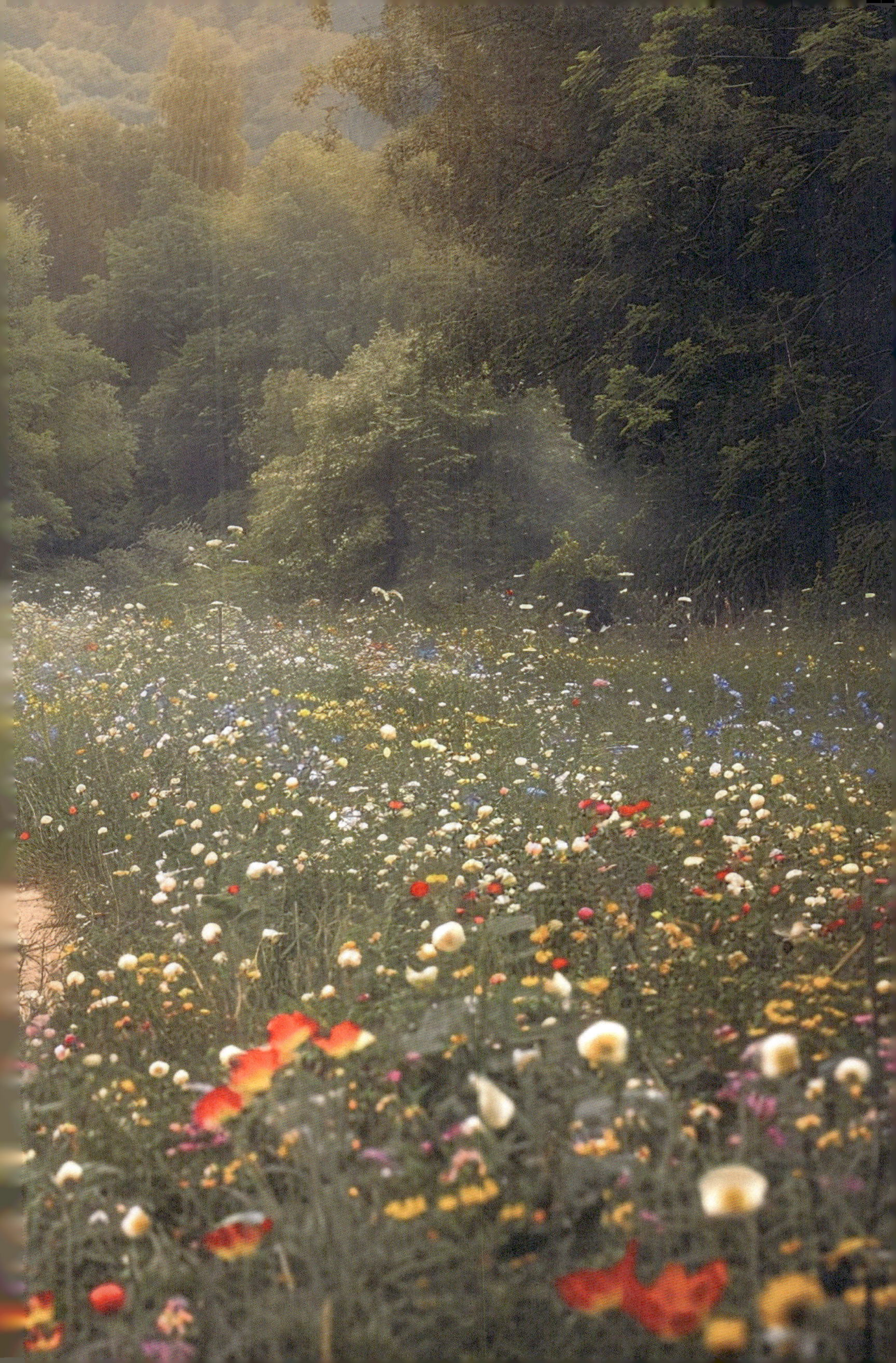

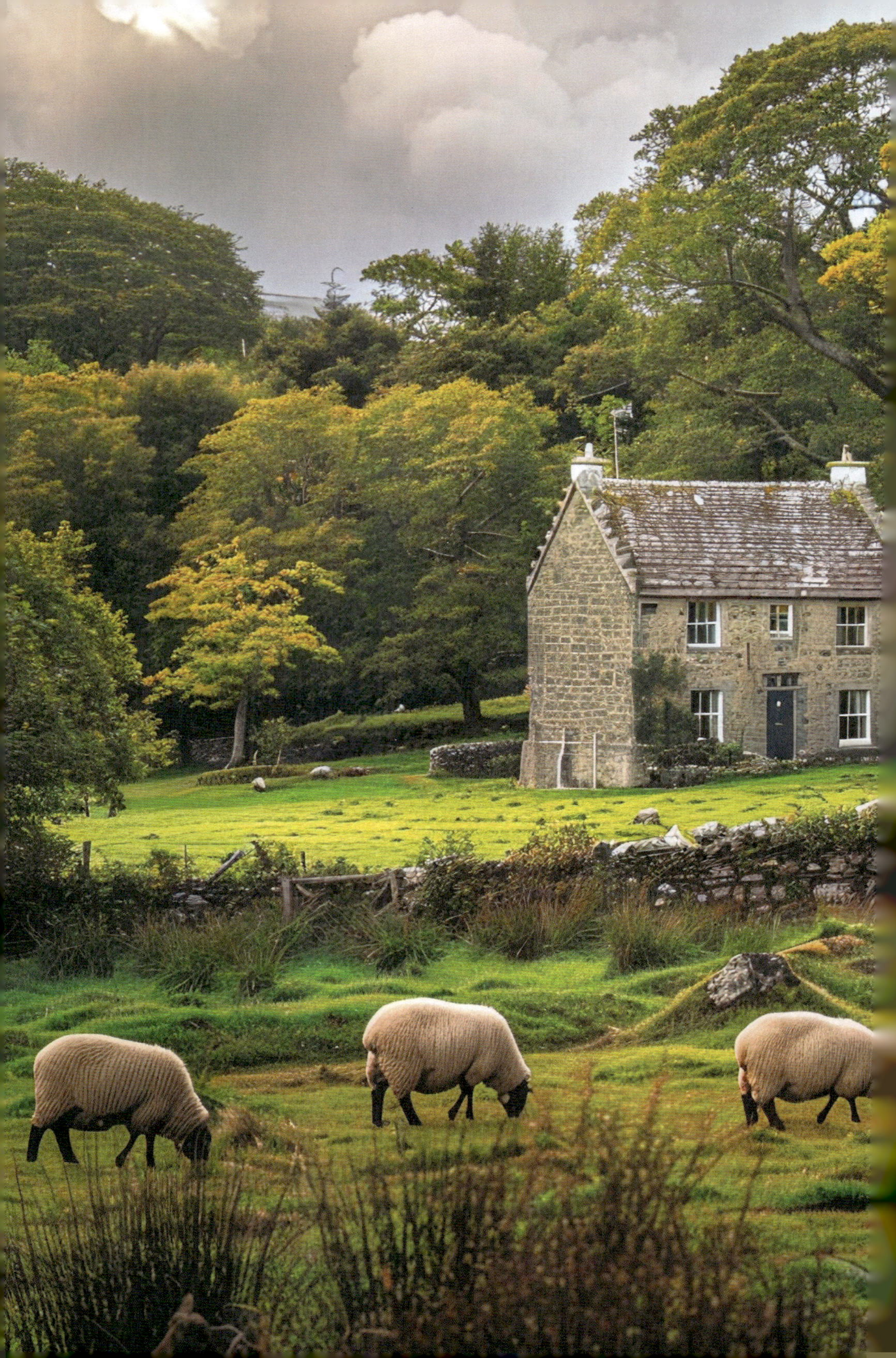

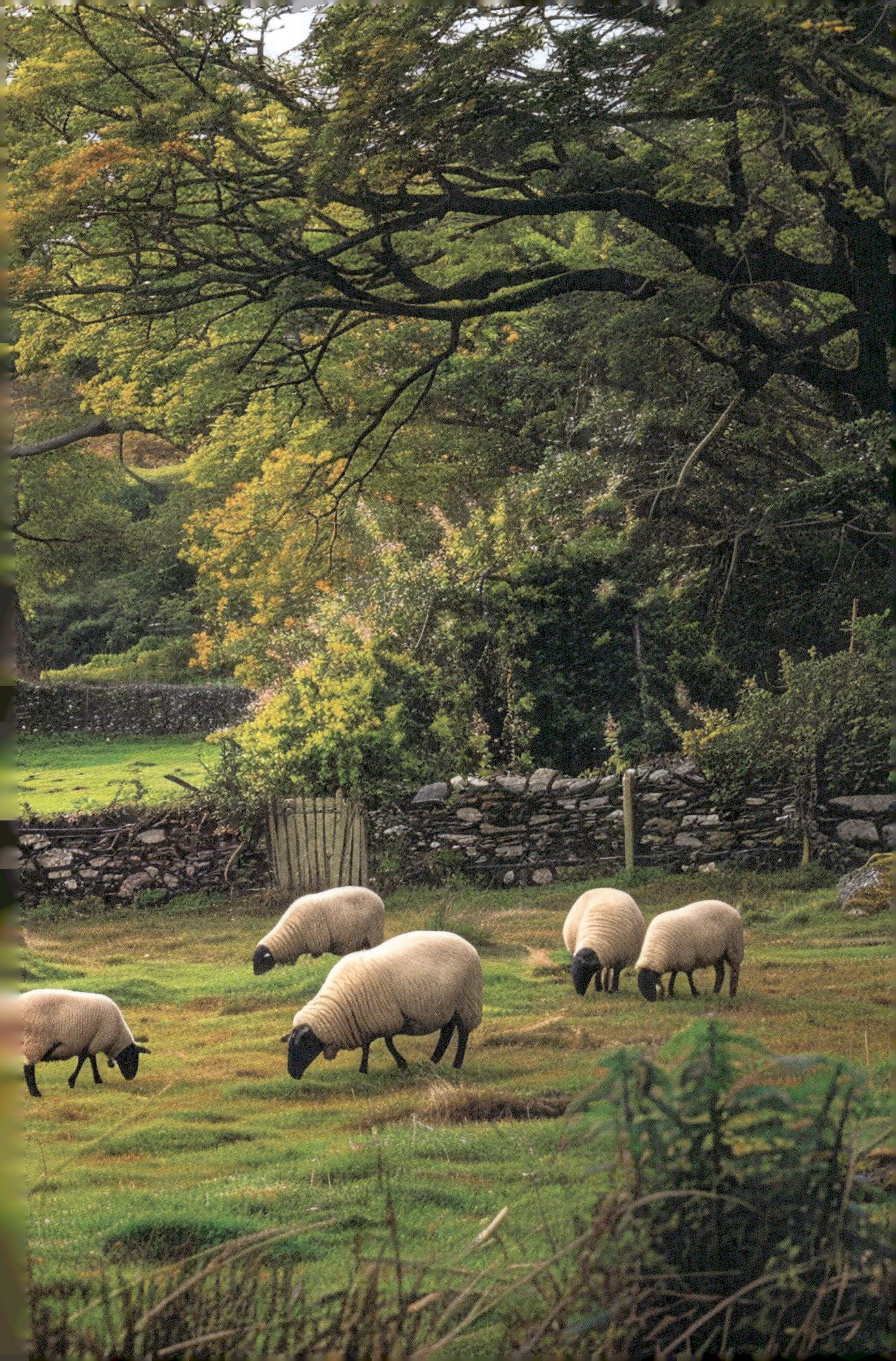

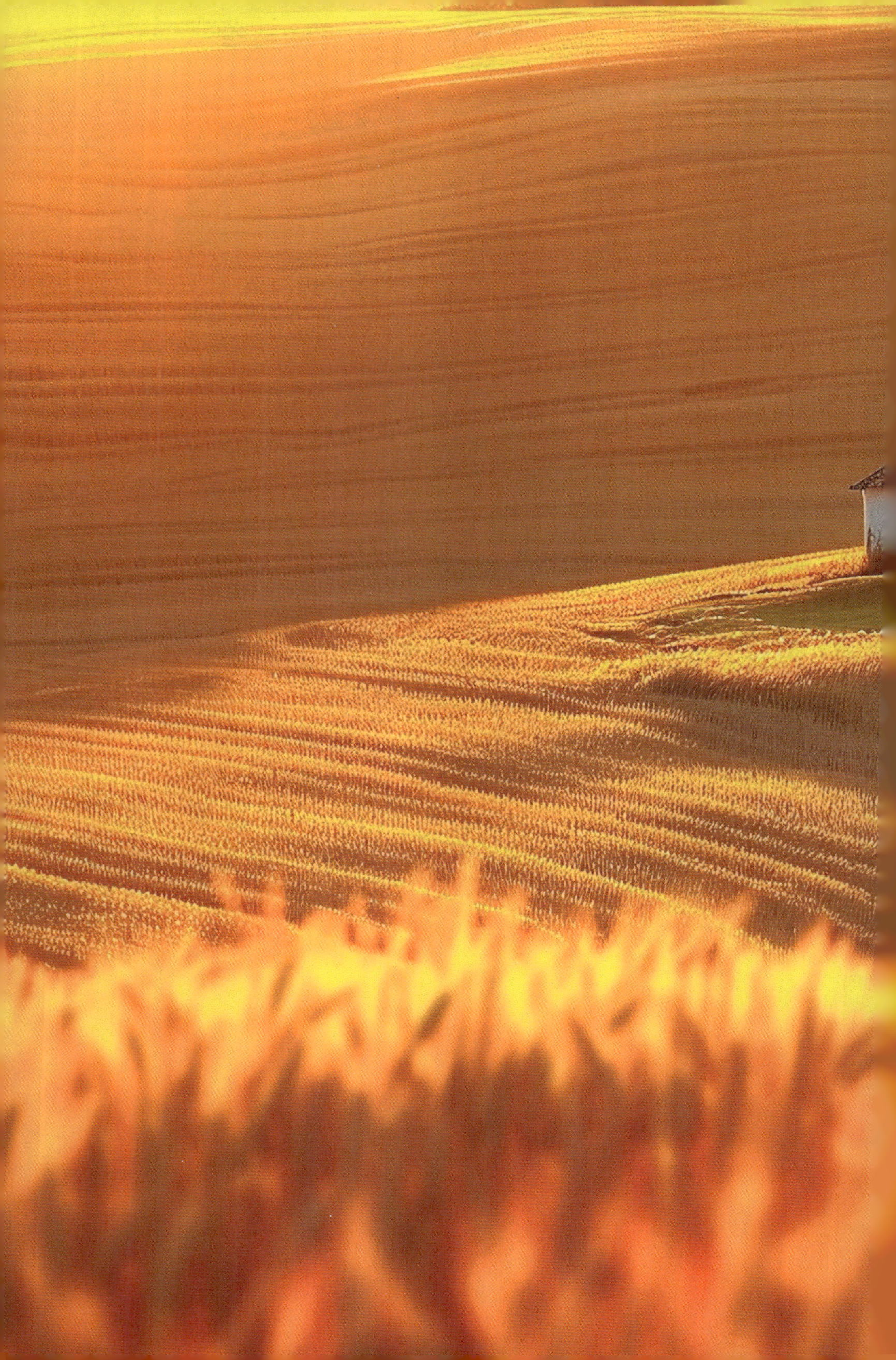

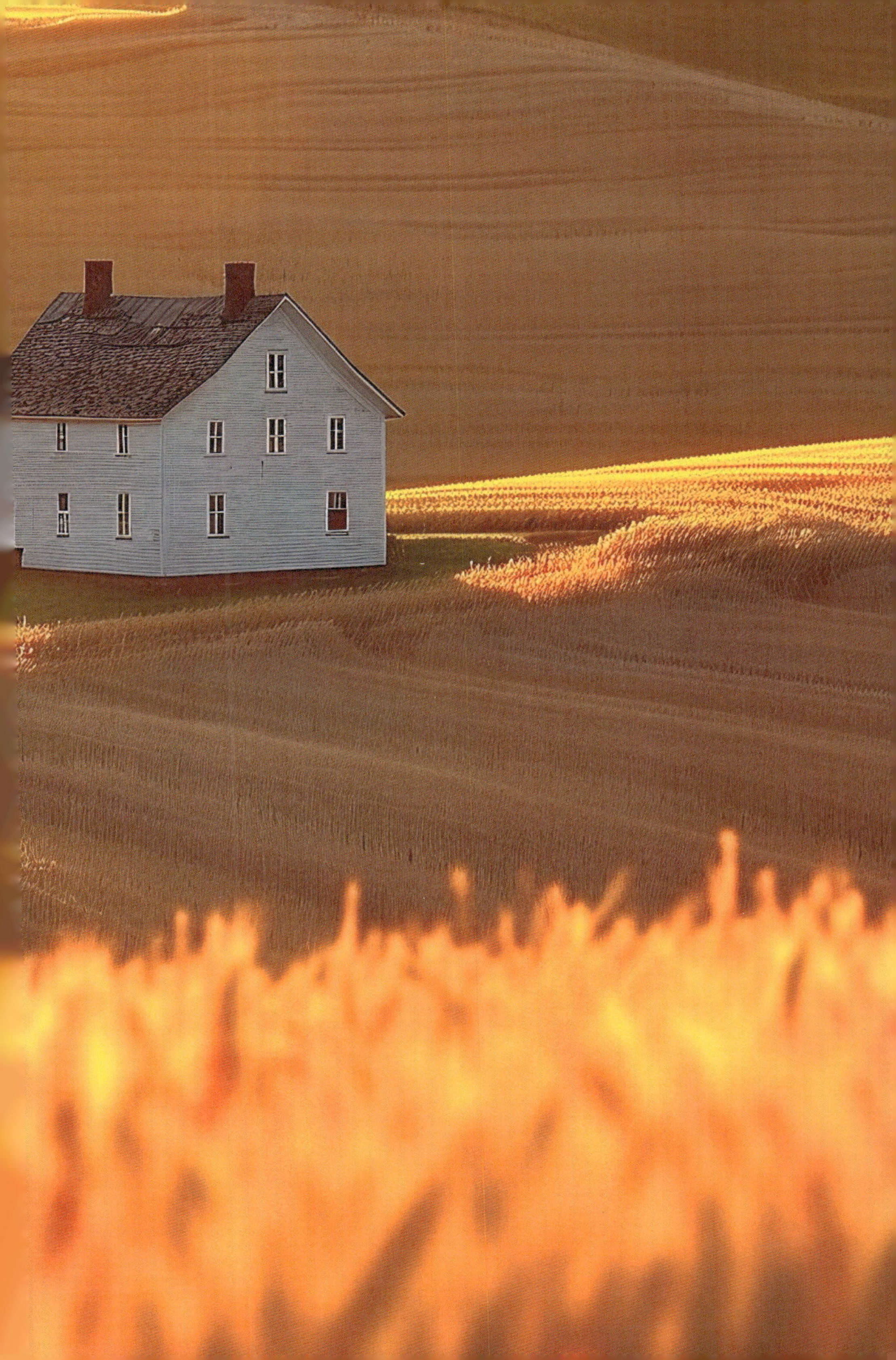

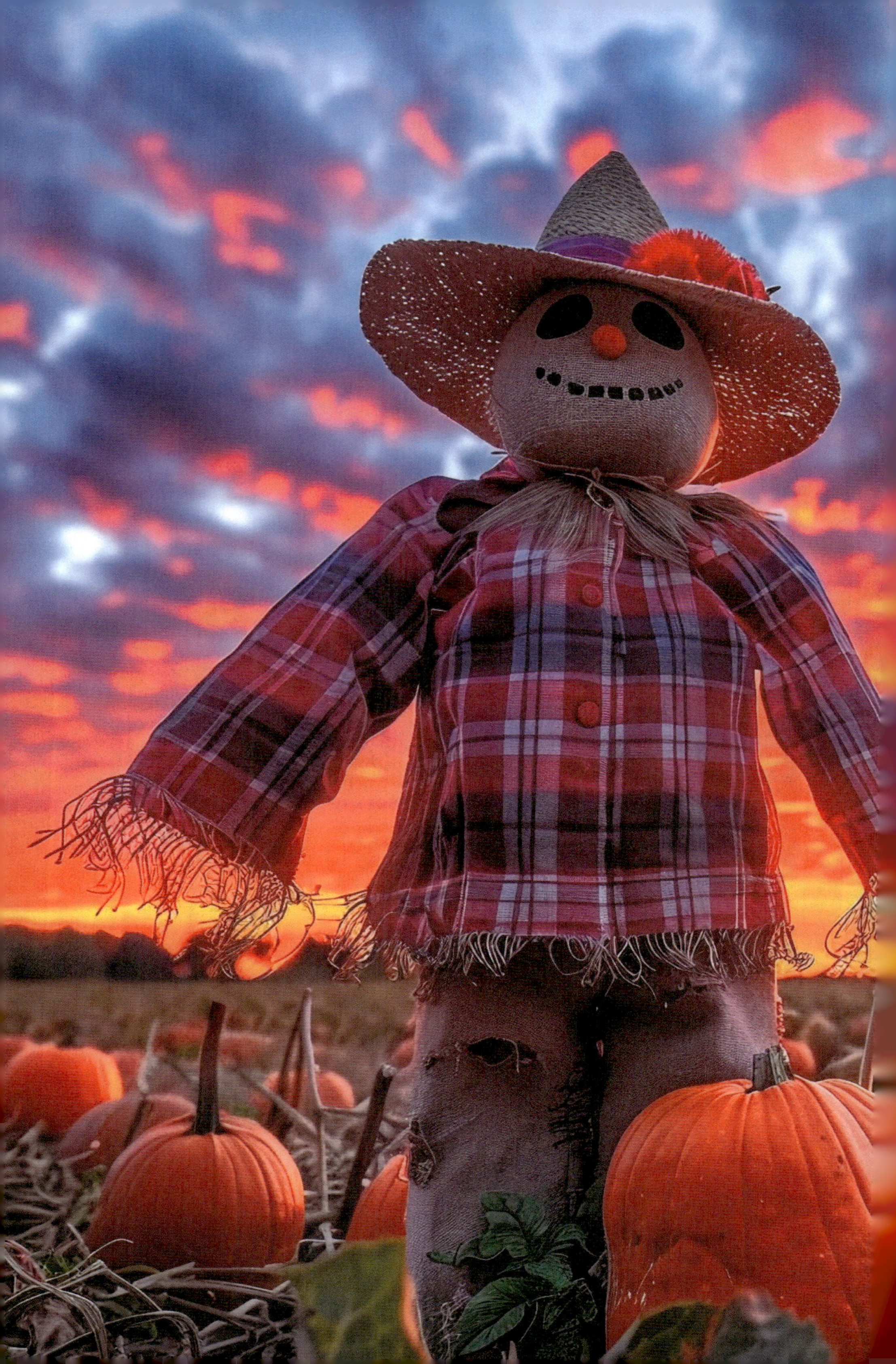

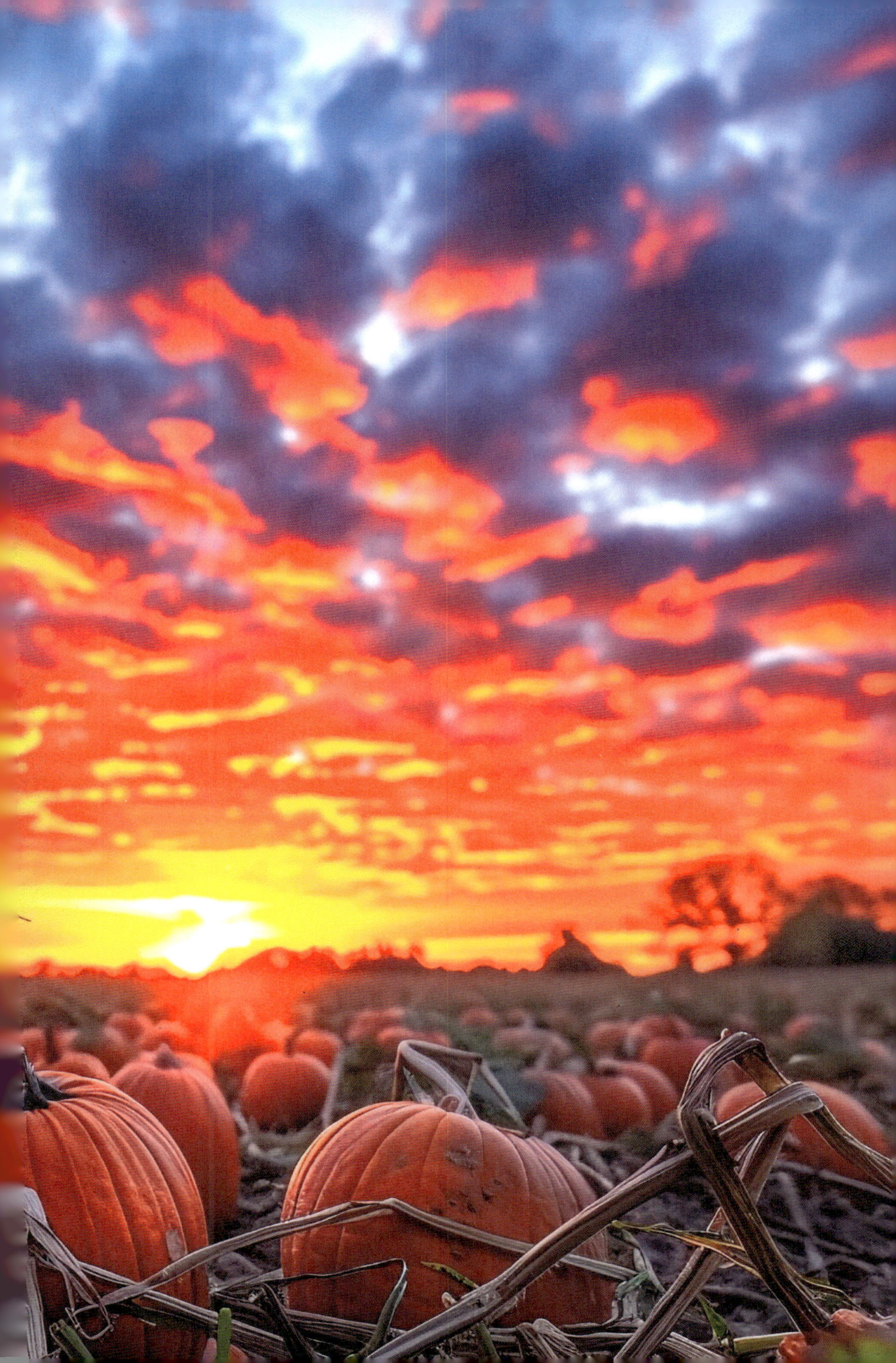

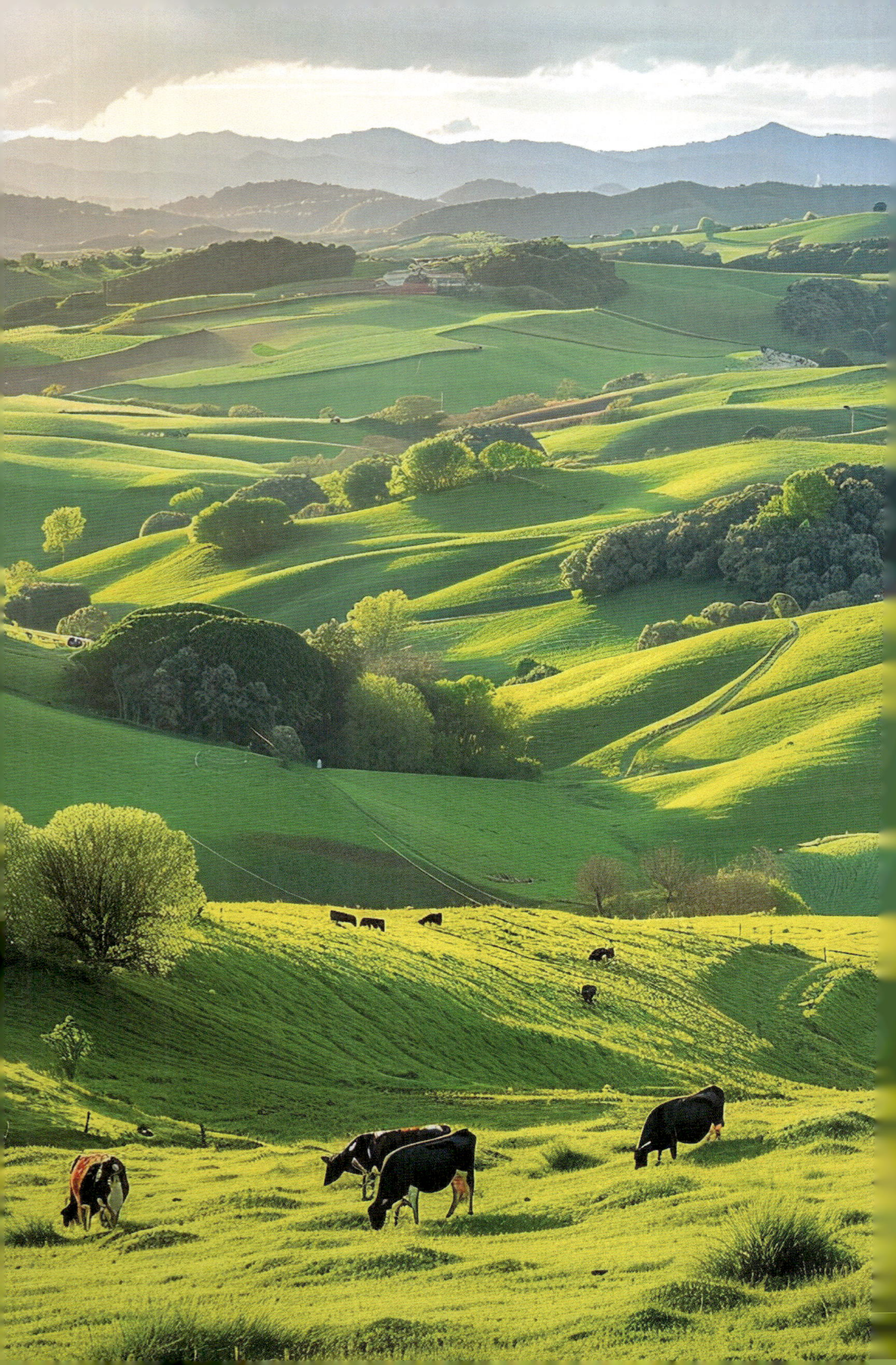

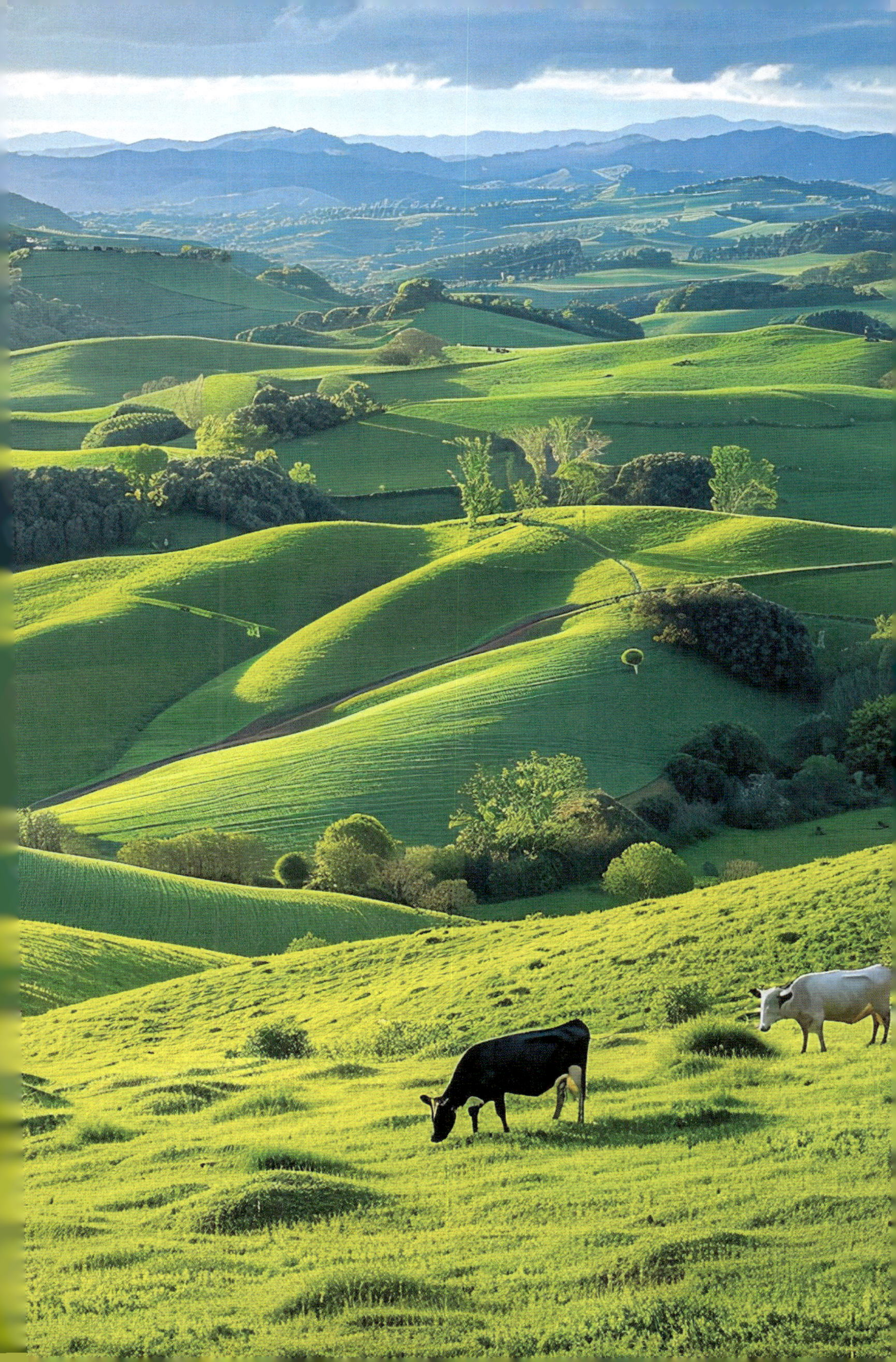

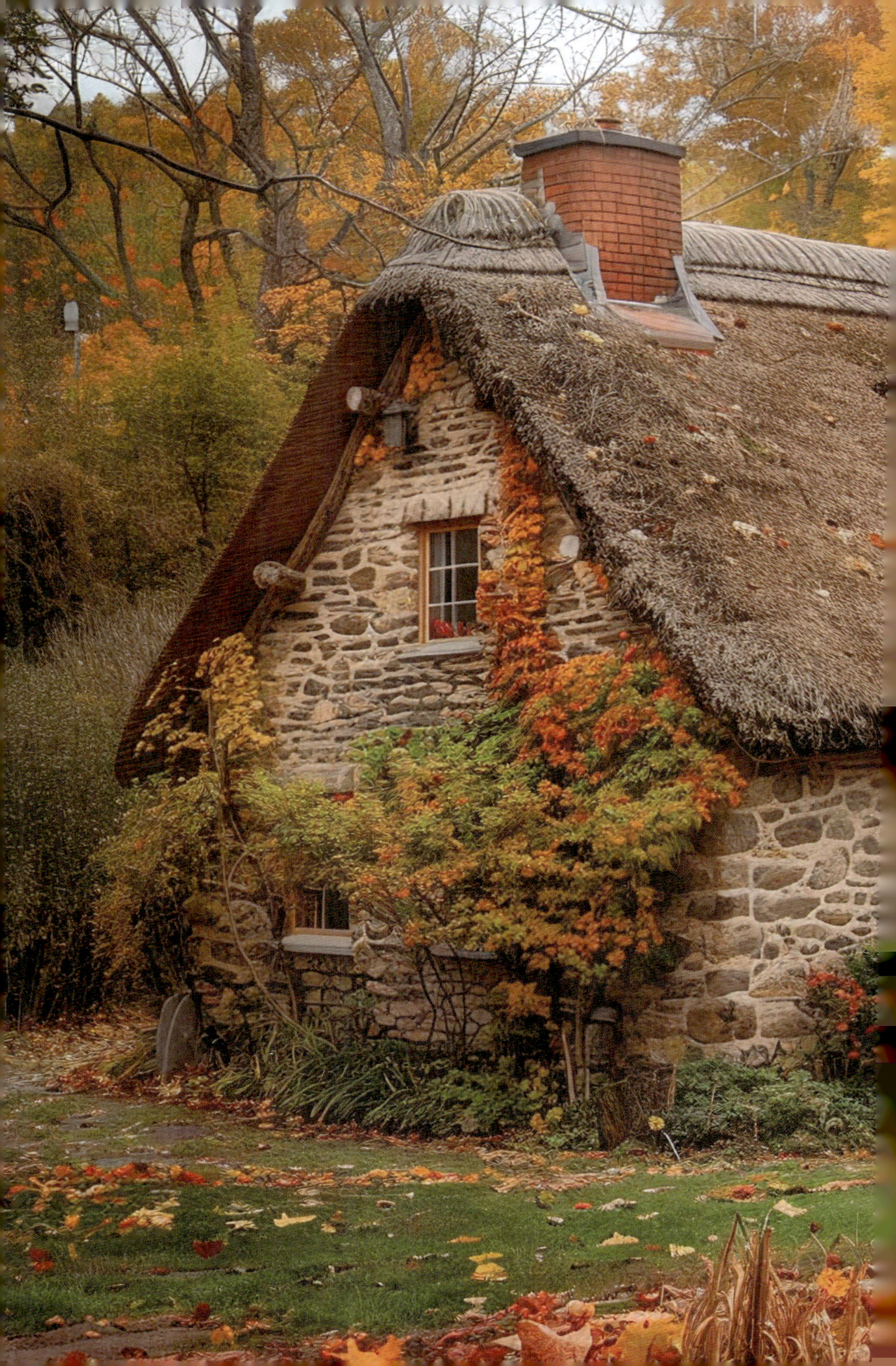

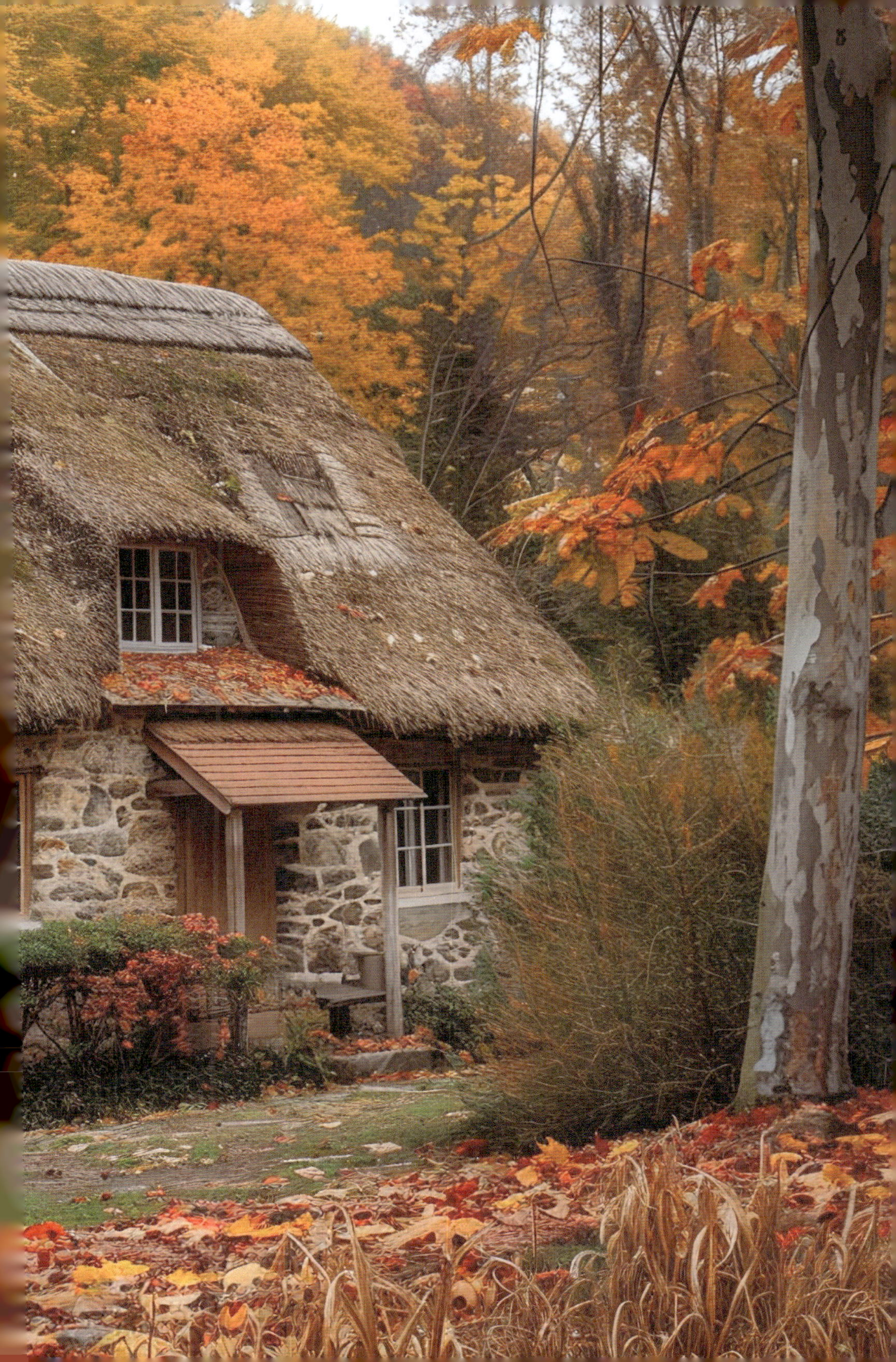

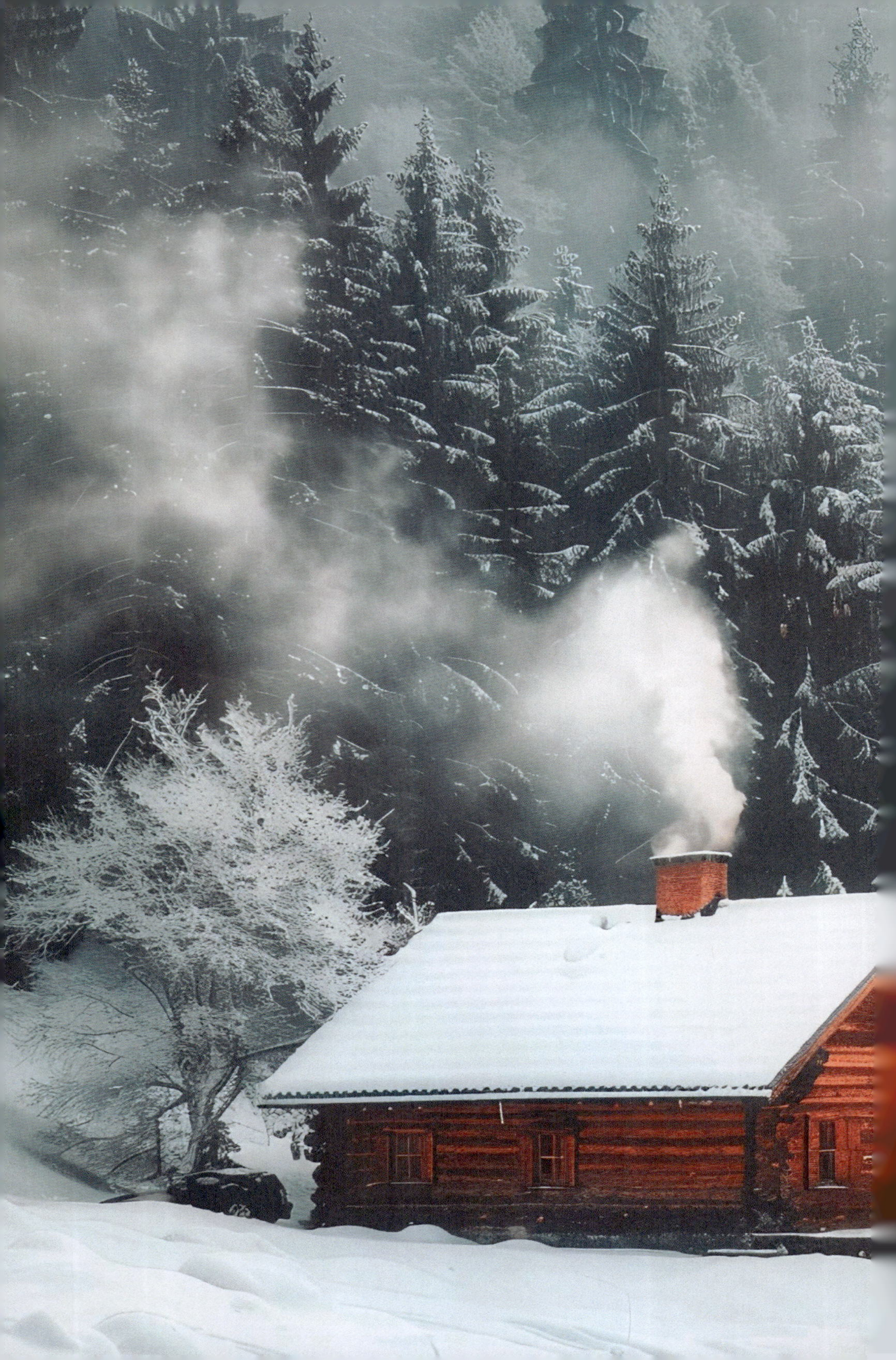

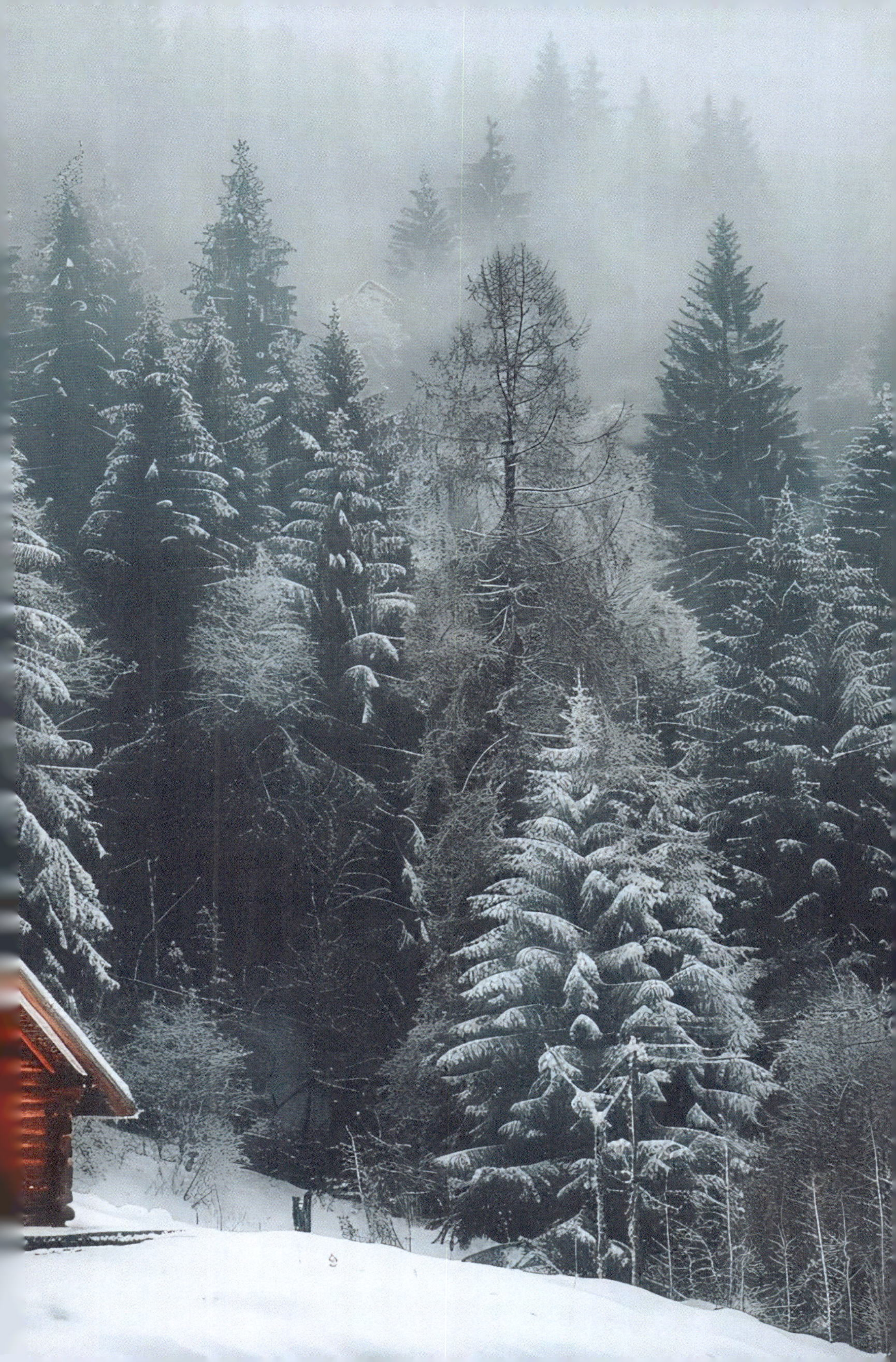

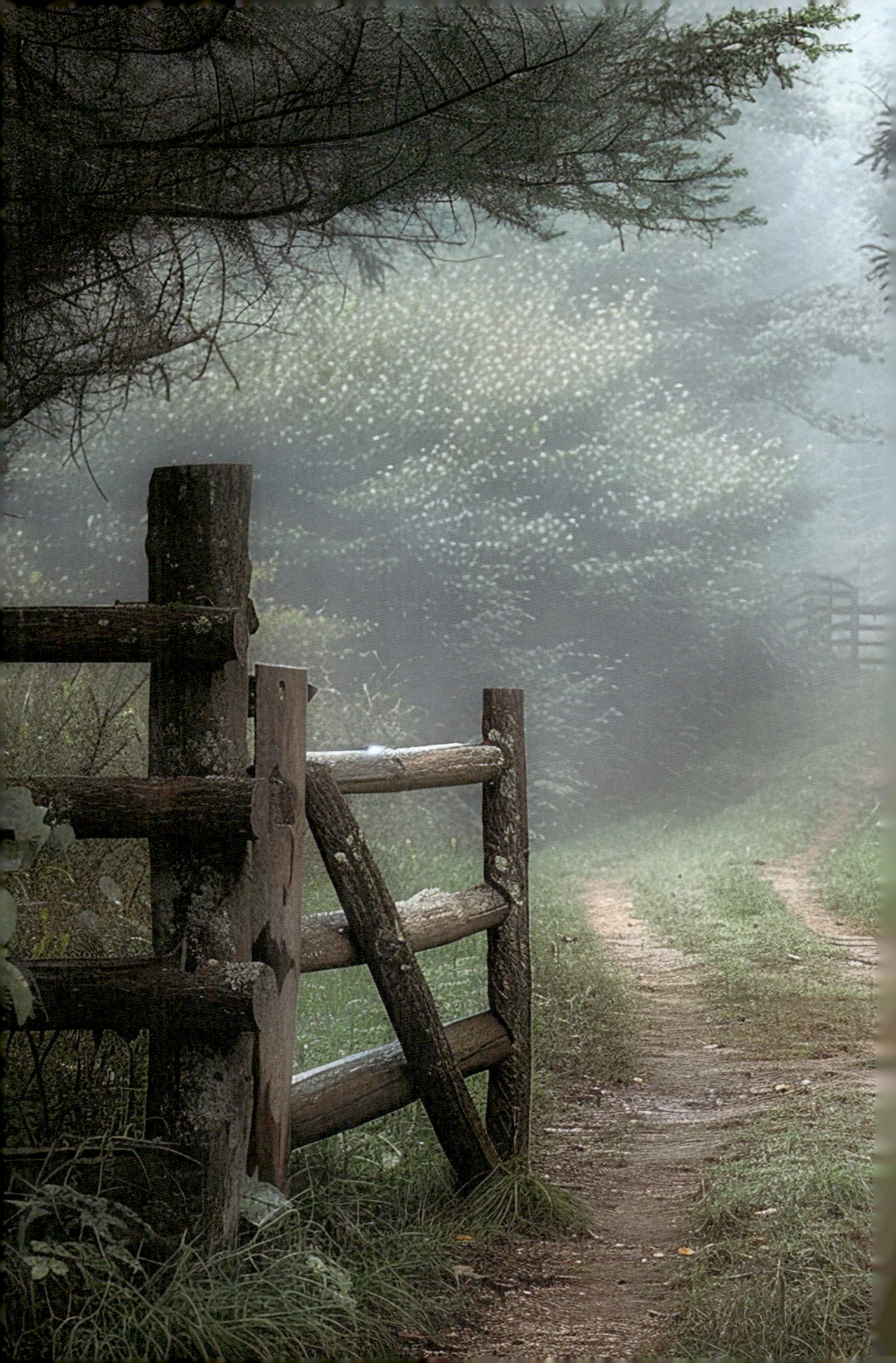

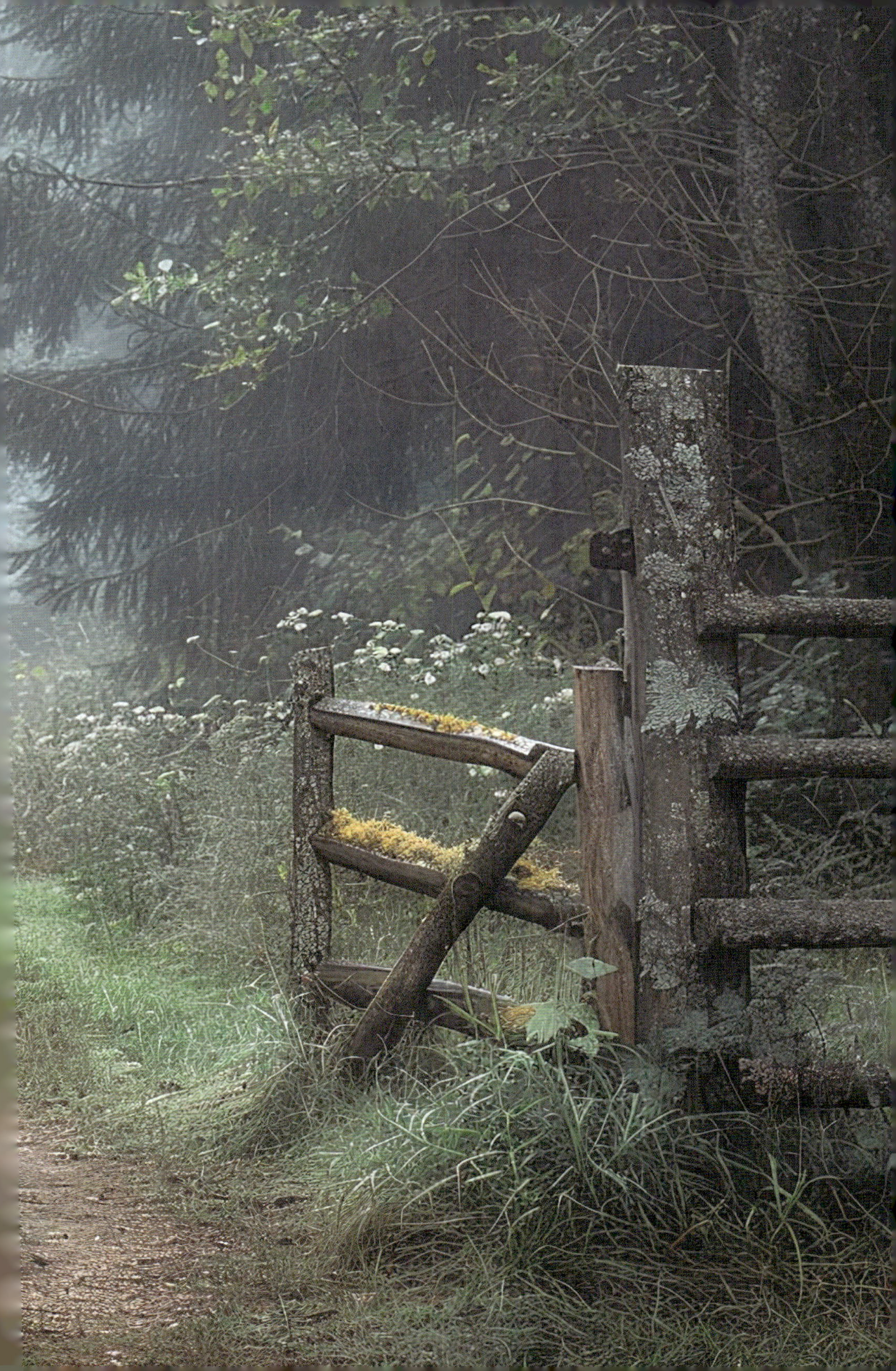

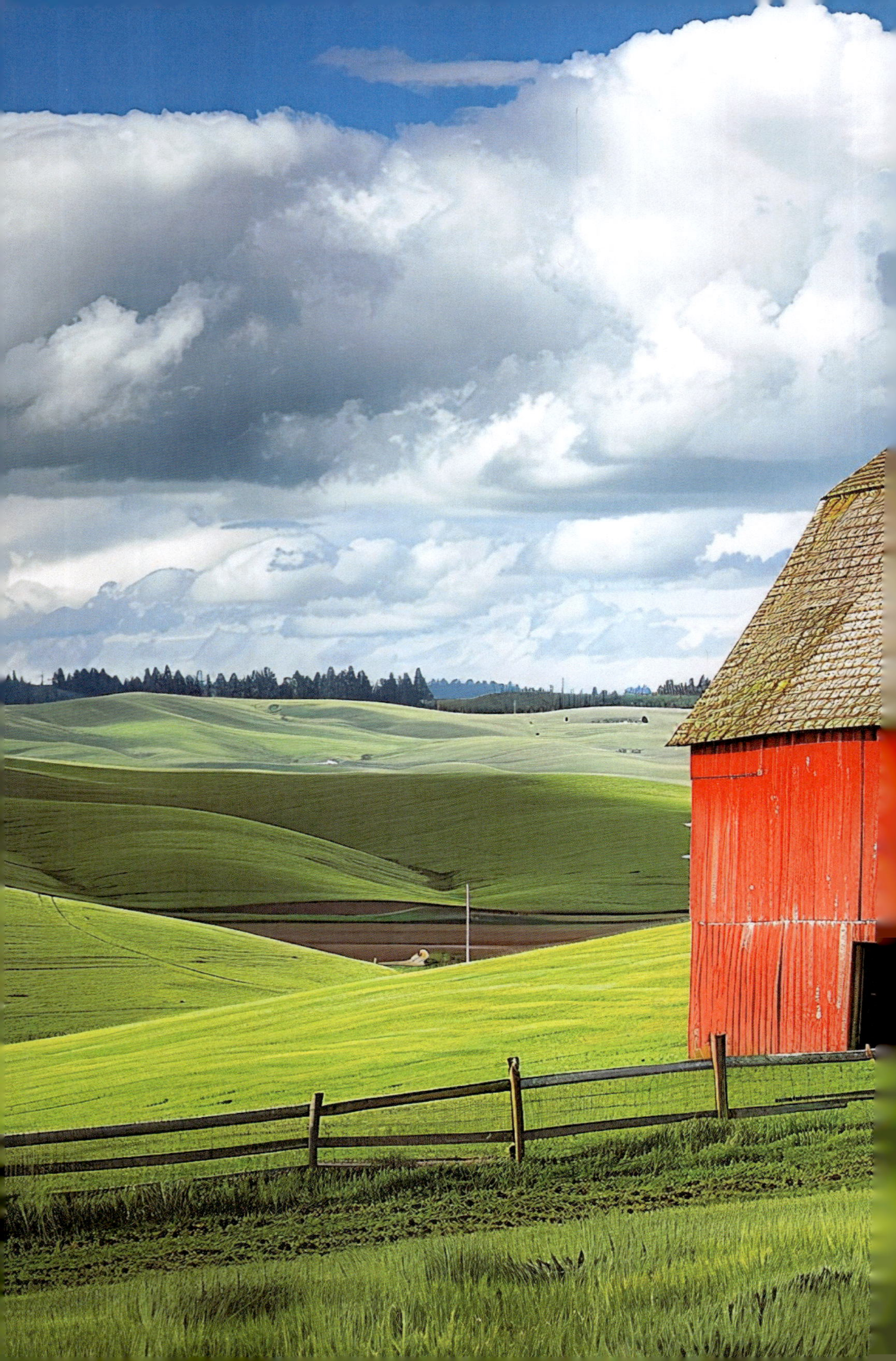

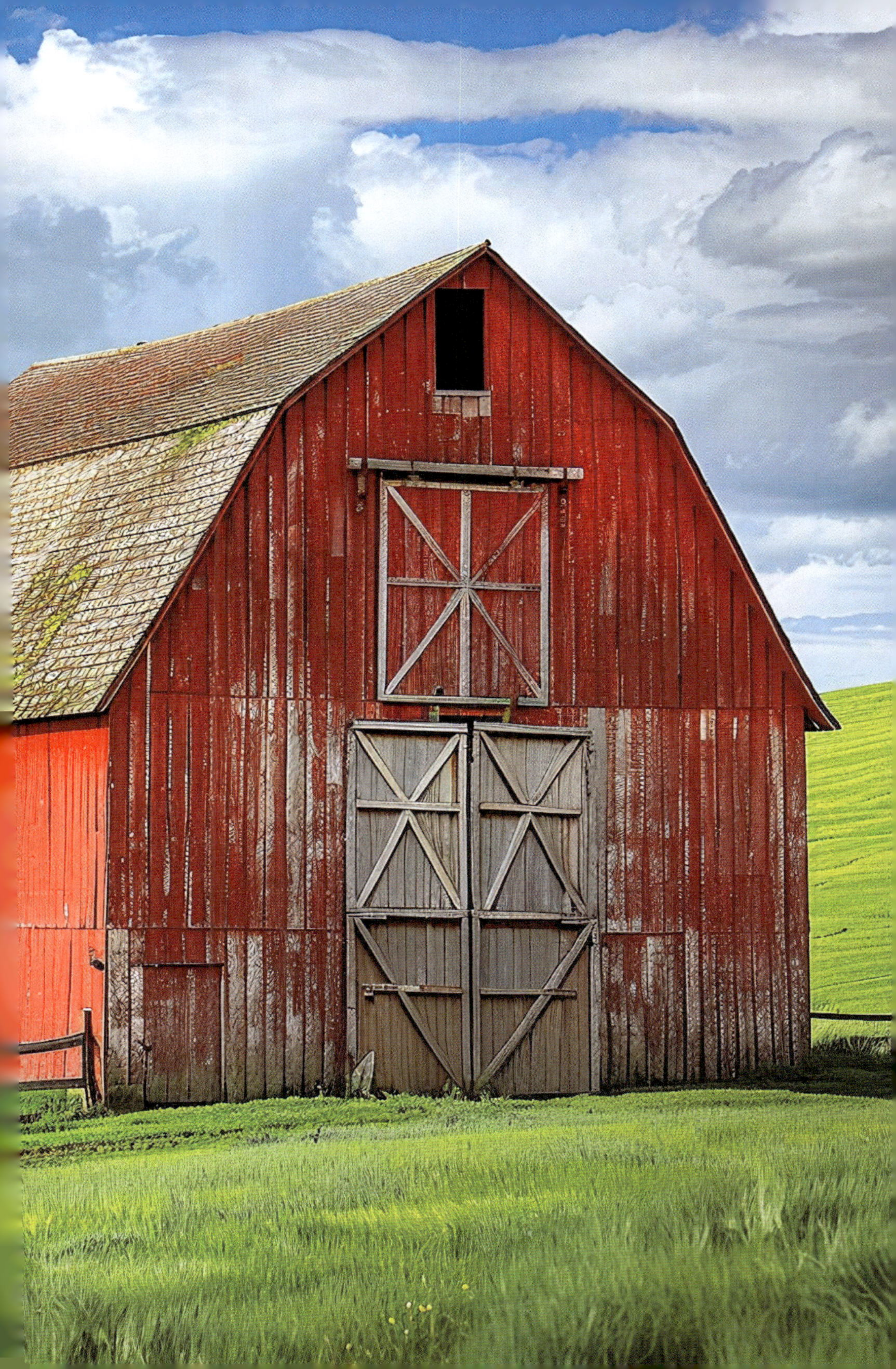

Printed in Great Britain
by Amazon

43948149R00025